★★★★★

GETTING ELECTED

is the

EASY PART

GETTING ELECTED
is the
EASY PART

WORKING AND WINNING
IN THE STATE LEGISLATURE

KAREN KEISER

WASHINGTON STATE SENATOR
PRESIDENT PRO TEMPORE

BASALT
BOOKS

Pullman, Washington

BASALT BOOKS

Basalt Books
PO Box 645910
Pullman, Washington 99164-5910
Phone: 800-354-7360
Email: basalt.books@wsu.edu
Website: basaltbooks.wsu.edu

DISCLAIMER: The publication of this work does not indicate an endorsement by Basalt Books or Washington State University of the author's political position or the views stated within. Basalt Books encourages authors of all viewpoints to submit their work for consideration.

Library of Congress Cataloging-in-Publication Data is available.

Basalt Books is an imprint of Washington State University Press.

The Washington State University Pullman campus is located on the homelands of the Niimíipuu (Nez Perce) Tribe and the Palus people. We acknowledge their presence here since time immemorial and recognize their continuing connection to the land, to the water, and to their ancestors. WSU Press is committed to publishing works that foster a deeper understanding of the Pacific Northwest and the contributions of its Native peoples.

Cover design by Patrick Brommer

DEDICATION

Dedicated to the thousands of state lawmakers who work to improve the health, safety, education, environment, economic security, equity, and opportunity for their constituents.

CONTENTS

FOREWORD

Liz Shuler
AFL-CIO PRESIDENT

Are you a newly elected member of your state legislature wondering what to do next? A political scientist or activist looking for an insider's perspective at the state level? This book is for you.

Building bridges with unlikely supporters, winning allies inside and outside the legislature, the power of perseverance—those are just a few pieces of practical guidance and wisdom in this treasure trove by veteran lawmaker Karen Keiser, the Washington State Senate President Pro Tempore.

Thousands of state lawmakers are elected every two years. After the elation of winning their first election, new lawmakers, especially women and people of color, don't always find a culture or the guidance to grow their passion and realize their aspirations. This book offers a practical guide to help new, and veteran, state legislators be effective and successful lawmakers.

While each state has its own traditions and procedures, the fundamentals are the same. This book clearly lays out how to navigate a complex legislative institution. Told with grace and humor, it shares the lived experience and vivid examples of a veteran lawmaker.

Karen also shows us, through the example of her service, the results we get when we elect pro-worker candidates. Karen is a long-time champion of working people and families. I met her through her work at the Washington State Labor Council when I was a young activist at my local union, and she was a source for wisdom and advice that put me on a leadership pathway in the labor movement. It was thrilling to see her rise in Washington politics and win a seat in the state senate in 2001. I watched with pride as she advanced laws that improved the lives of working families throughout the state.

In 2002, Karen introduced the first paid sick leave bill in her state. Critics laughed, but Karen persisted—and today mandatory sick leave is the law in Washington state. Her leadership had a positive spillover effect. Following Washington's example, other states have adopted variations of the law.

Passing progressive legislation state by state doesn't always get the big headlines. It's not easy, and it doesn't attract a lot of praise. But where proposals stall on the federal level, state legislators like Karen make all the difference in the world for millions of working families. This book successfully argues why state legislatures should never be overlooked as powerful allies and partners for progress. As president of the AFL-CIO, I see and hear from working people all across our economy the impact policies like paid family leave, project labor agreements, and expanded health care have at the state level.

A state-based approach is critical now and for the future. It's how we can make progress for working families, climate resilience, gender equity, racial and social justice, voting rights—and so much more. As former Speaker of the U.S. House of Representatives Tip O'Neill famously observed so long ago, "All politics is local." For a no-nonsense primer on how to turn local politics into successful policy, read *Getting Elected is the Easy Part: Working and Winning in the State Legislature.*

My friend, Elise Bryant, president of the Coalition of Labor Union Women, often uses these words to motivate audiences: "We did not come this far to give up now."

Standing on the shoulders of legislator giants like Karen, it's time for the next generation to build on so much hard-won progress. Karen's book is the perfect guide for showing us exactly how to do that.

PROLOGUE

"We move from one crisis to another. We suffer one disturbance and shock after another." So said Sir Austen Chamberlain, who described himself as a very old Parliamentarian, in 1936. He is purported to have referenced what he called an old curse, "May you live in interesting times," the original source of which cannot not be verified.

For today's state lawmakers, that old curse may well be coming true. Despite the confirmation of U.S. Supreme Court Justice Ketanji Brown Jackson (KBJ), the first Black woman appointed to our nation's highest judiciary, the court appears to be reversing course on several foundational issues and is referring many disputes back to the states.

In 2022, the Supreme Court concluded its session with a series of historic decisions: repealing the constitutional right to abortion granted by *Roe v. Wade*, 410 U.S. 113 (1973) in its *Dobbs v. Jackson Women's Health Organization*, 592 U.S. (2022) decision and, in its *West Virginia v. Environmental Protection Agency*, 597 U.S. (2022) decision, revoking the federal agency's authority to curtail power plant emissions to delay climate change. The court sent the issues of abortion and air pollution to the states for action.

In that same term, the court repealed a century-old New York state gun law limiting the right to carry guns outside the home. The *New York State Rifle & Pistol Association, Inc. v. Bruen*, 59 U.S. (2022) ruling also automatically repeals similar laws in California, Hawaii, Maryland, Massachusetts, and New Jersey. (In a swift reaction, New York's governor called a special session of the legislature to enact new laws restricting locations of where people can carry guns, such as schools and government buildings. A few days later, New Jersey's governor signed new laws requiring gun training and gun registration of out-of-state firearms.)[1]

With many states passing laws on same-sex marriage and transgender issues, ensuing lawsuits may well open the door for the Supreme Court to overturn its *Obergefell v. Hodges*, 576, U.S. 644 (2015) ruling that established a constitutional right to same-sex marriage. As with the abortion case, more than two dozen states already have state laws on the books restricting transgender people and same-sex marriage. It does seem the days of stare decisis, or settled law and respect for precedent, are over.

The renewed tug of war between the states and the federal government is part of our country's heritage. In 1857, the Supreme Court's awful *Dred Scott v. Sandford* decision on slavery set the table for the Civil War. The current court seems to favor state legislative action on issues it deems non-constitutional while restricting state action on issues, such as guns and religion, that it deems requiring constitutional protection.

It certainly makes for "interesting times" to be a state lawmaker. Creative strategies and coordinating on progressive state laws on contentious issues may further divide us. But if the federal government cannot ensure a national standard for laws on fundamental education, health, safety, climate, and social issues, it will be imperative for state legislatures to do what they can to protect their constituents.

The onset of the COVID-19 pandemic made clear a harsh new reality for America: our federal government could no longer be relied upon to preserve public health and safety. Key elements of our federal government possessed neither the leadership nor the commitment to place our common good ahead of ideology or loyalty to Donald Trump. In 2021, the Supreme Court again weighed in to restrict the federal Occupational Safety and Health Administration (OSHA) from mandating that large employers require employees to either get a COVID-19 test or a vaccination. In the face of this epic failure at the federal level, many proactive and productive state governments took responsible and dramatic action to protect their residents.[2]

Our country's state legislatures are different in many ways but all have the capacity to act to defend or improve the lives of the people who voted them into office. I am privileged to serve in the Washington State Legislature. I wrote this book as a kind of manual or guide for newly elected lawmakers who want to take positive action at the state level. I am encouraged by the new young lawmakers being elected in recent years, especially women and people of color who for so long were not represented in our chambers. I hope I can help them achieve their goals by sharing my story and my observations and lived experience.

Progress is often difficult but always possible. For example, as the chair of the Senate Health Care Committee some years back, I advocated for state policies that anticipated the Affordable Care Act (ACA) and moved to quickly expand Medicaid and adopt other measures at the state level to enact the ACA's benefits as soon as it passed. It was not a coincidence that our state Health Benefit Exchange was able to implement the ACA far more quickly and efficiently than other states—we had either proactively implemented key components or prepared for their implementation while other states deferred to the federal program. More recently, our legislature voted to write into state law key benefits under the Affordable Care Act so that, even if action is taken at the federal level to repeal protections and coverage, health care policies in Washington will continue to honor the standards of the ACA.

According to a 2020 report, "Congress at a Crossroads," produced by the Association of Former Members of Congress, "Congress has largely become a dysfunctional institution unable to meet the critical needs of our country."[3] The report's authors admit to the lack of a magic wand to fix the mess in Congress.[4] Our state legislatures, however, may well have some answers.

Until now, state legislatures have been treated like junior league political footballs by much of the political cognoscenti of our country. Mostly they're looked at as a means to an end, the end being control of redistricting.

Karl Rove and his wildly successful 2010 GOP Redistricting Majority Project aimed to win more than a hundred legislative seats in sixteen states where redistricting maps were drawn by the majority in power in the state's legislatures.[5] Not coincidentally, while Democrats focused on the White House and Congress, they lost nearly 1,000 legislative seats while Obama was in office. In 2022, Republicans controlled thirty bicameral state legislatures while Democrats held only sixteen. Three states had a divided legislature, which is usually a recipe for impasse.[6]

Democrats held the majority of state legislatures for only five of the past twenty years—in 2003 and from 2008 through 2011. Rove's red-state strategy is why so many states had trigger laws in place to ban abortions as soon as the Supreme Court overturned *Roe v. Wade.*

It's past time for a smarter strategy. So why not consider state legislatures as partners where progressive policies can be tested and perfected? Without a coordinated strategy among blue states working to advance issues such as climate change, racial justice, and police reform—and better labor and health standards— we lose the experience and knowledge gained by the real-world implementation of progressive policies. Consider it an opportunity to field test new ideas. For America and its people, political power should be used to make the best choices.

Each of our fifty state governments and legislatures is unique. State legislatures have no easy process for coordination or cooperation, given their wide ranges of political leanings, capacities, and traditions. The National Council of State Legislatures tries mightily to keep the big tent open, and other more regional and aligned groups from the Council of State Governments to Women in Government provide forums for valuable dialogue. Advocacy groups, such as ALEC and SiX also weigh in, but none truly wade through the weeds of legislative processes.

As a progressive, I was moved by the reality of our country's political alignment over the last twenty years to look at what our state legislatures have done and could do to make significant progress. In particular, I focused on what we could do if the federal government failed to act on important issues—from paid family and medical leave, to voting rights and fair campaign laws. States have led the way forward for millions of Americans and made their lives better. Conversely, and sadly, these are all areas where our federal government has not led in some time.

I searched but could not find any book that provides the practical and political knowledge to help young lawmakers achieve their goals and make real change—especially for newly-elected women and people of color. The time-honored and woefully outdated "good old boys'" culture appears to still be the default in too many legislatures across our nation.

You can find books, classes, and online instruction in political campaign tactics, campaign training courses, and campaign plans, biographies and auto-biographies, and civics texts to no end. But you won't find much advice at all on the sausage making of lawmaking. To that end, I hope this contribution will help fill that gap. This is not a page-turner. It's more a kind of reference book of shared personal and professional observations and lived experience.

The legislative process is arcane and often mystifying. There's lots to learn to become effective. Each state has its own traditions and rules. And each new legislator has to choose their own path and create their own niche. But—and I know this to be true—if you hold on to your core values and persist, you, too, can change the world one state at a time.

That's not hyperbole.

NOTES

1. Matt Vasilogambros, "Supreme Court's Gun Rights Decision Upends State Restrictions." *Stateline*, July 8, 2022. https://www.pewtrusts.org/en/research-and-analysis/blogs/stateline/2022/07/08/supreme-courts-gun-rights-decision-upends-state-restrictions.

2. In April 2023, *The Lancet* published an analysis showing Washington state had the sixth lowest COVID death rate in the United States, with 286 deaths per 100,000—about 23 percent lower than the national average. See Bollyky, Thomas J. et al., "Assessing CO-VID-19 pandemic policies and behaviours and their economic and educational trade-offs across US states from Jan 1, 2020, to July 31, 2022: an observational analysis," *The Lancet*, Volume 401, Issue 10385, 1341–1360. https://doi.org/10.1016/S0140-6736(23)0.

3. Association of Former Members of Congress, "Congress at a Crossroads," www.usafmc.org/congressxroads.

4. Carl Hulse, "Congress Has Become a Toxic Mess. Can it be Saved?" *New York Times*, July 26, 2020.

5. Joan Walsh, "The 7,383-Seat Strategy," *The Nation*, September 7, 2020.

6. Nebraska has a unicameral legislature with a Republican majority.

CHAPTER 1

What Was I Thinking?

"We hold these truths to be self-evident, that all men and women are created equally."
—Elizabeth Cady Stanton

I was a middle-aged, white, working mom with three kids, a rocky marriage, and a demanding full-time job in communications. What possessed me to throw my name into the ring for an open seat in the state legislature? Looking back, it made sense. But at the time, it seemed plain crazy.

Twenty-five years later—omigod, a quarter of a century—I decided it was time to share my experiences and observations in hopes that others elected to a tradition-bound (some might say hidebound) legislative body could use my discoveries and "aha!" moments to ease their own paths forward. It's an eternal plaint: "If I had known then what I know now…"

I grew up in a very small Iowa farming town where my father owned the general store. My mom and dad worked seven days a week with only Sunday afternoons off. That left me and my sisters and brother fairly unfettered, except for when we, too, worked at the store. I spent days behind the old-fashioned fountain, making hot fudge sundaes, Green River sodas, and malted milk shakes. But many other days I was free to wander and explore. It was a marvelous childhood. Sunday mornings meant church with afternoons spent with grandparents, having Sunday dinner where the talk circled around the latest episode of *Meet the Press*. Politics was on the table right next to the pot roast and potatoes.

Prairie populism was my heritage. My grandfather was a wealthy farmer in the roaring 1920s, but when the Depression hit, the bank foreclosed on his farm, and he kept food on the table by toiling as a grave digger. My grandmother stopped Grampa Keiser from murdering the town banker, according to family lore: when he took off for town with his shotgun, she corralled him from making it all the way to the bank. Knowing Grandma Blanche, I wouldn't put it past her. Stern would be a charitable adjective in her case.

My father spent much of the Great Depression at the state university, which then was almost tuition free in South Dakota. He claimed to have eaten fried potatoes and jam for four years to make ends meet in college. On the side, he played trombone and picked up gigs, at one point performing at the Chicago World's Fair as a member of the South Dakota state band. He said he turned down a chance to join the Lawrence Welk band because he couldn't stand the corny "a one and a two" music they played.

My mother taught in the county school, which back then didn't require a college education. She was smart and sassy and always said she thought she had been born fifty years too early, as she really was a women's libber in her heart. Both my parents fully enjoyed life and each other, and I felt fortunate to grow up in a loving, lively family.

No life is without challenges. But mine was blessed with a fundamental faith that things would work out somehow. It was the era of the American Dream, when parents expected their kids to succeed, and the impetus from my parents was a Samsonite suitcase upon my graduation from high school. Message: time to move out. And off I went.

Then came the Vietnam War and the civil rights and women's liberation movements of the 1960s. In college, at University of California, Berkeley, I studied political science—academically in the classroom and firsthand in the streets, where the stringent smell of tear gas often hung above Telegraph Avenue. I was lucky to get through my studies without being arrested, as the tough Oakland police force seemed ever present at every demonstration and protest.

Next up, a "third-rate burglary" that came to be known as Watergate. It was an intoxicating time. As I watched it all unfold, I decided to become a reporter and "comfort the afflicted and afflict the comfortable," in the inspiring news philosophy of the day.[1]

Going to journalism school honed my skills. Working as a reporter opened my eyes. On the first day on my first job as a TV reporter in Portland, Oregon, I watched a young woman jump to her death from a downtown department store. It was horrifying and disturbing. We didn't show the film on the news that night. In those days, editors were taught to exercise restraint. These days it would be posted on YouTube and go viral within minutes.

As a TV reporter, I saw and smelled death and destruction. I dug into corruption at the Pierce County Sheriff's Office, but I also laughed and enjoyed the delightful people about us. Reporting the epic eruption of Mount St. Helens and its aftermath capped my career; nothing that followed seemed anywhere near as intense.

My husband and I wanted to start a family, so transitioning to a more predictable line of work made sense. I found a perfect fit in a new job as the communications director for the state AFL-CIO, where politics and my affinity for unions came together. My father had been a union member of the Insurance Workers Union (UFCW) when he worked as an agent for Prudential Insurance after World War II, and I had been a shop steward for my TV union, now known as SAG-AFTRA. Unions were under great stress following the recent firing of air traffic controllers by President Reagan, which had signaled a green light to union-busting efforts across the country.[2] We organized, held rallies and political events, and struggled to hold on in the ensuing years.

Back home, we had adopted our first child and had two more children. We had a comfortable middle-class life well underway with our little family in a suburban ranch house outside of Seattle.

We had a scare when our eighteen-month-old daughter's appendix burst and she spent weeks in intensive care with peritonitis, but she recovered fully and the kids were all healthy and mostly happy. My husband became interested in making documentaries; I became the chief bread winner with a steady paycheck and good benefits. In the ensuing years we grew apart, as his film making took him away for months at a time, and I struggled to manage the children and my job without much support.

So what in the hell was I thinking when I decided to throw my name into the ring when the incumbent state representative of my legislative district resigned to run for higher office? I had joined my local Democratic Party district organization (though I rarely attended meetings) and had volunteered to be a precinct committee officer (PCO). Even though I wasn't in the inner circle of the district organization, I knew some of the other PCOs—which was important since PCOs are the individuals who have a vote when it is time to send a replacement legislator to Olympia between elections. I had volunteered as my local PTA's legislative delegate, and my reporter job gave me access to a lot of political information. But overall, I was a newbie to running for office.

There were several other candidates vying for the position, which meant I wouldn't have to go directly against any one candidate and could hopefully split the vote. We had a town hall debate where I was delighted to see that the president of the State Labor Council had made his way to the meeting to speak on my behalf. Putting together a coalition of union and women's rights PCOs gave me the votes needed to be appointed to the seat for the 1995 session. It wasn't a big majority, but it was enough to win the seat after three rounds of PCO voting.

The timing was significant. Democrats had just suffered an awful rout, nationally and locally, and Newt Gingrich became the first Republican Speaker of the U.S. House of Representatives in four decades.[3] Democrats had lost the majority in the Washington State House of Representatives as well, for the first time in decades. When I arrived in Olympia for the 1995 legislative session, the Democratic caucus was in a state of trauma and shock.

The minority leader, Representative (now Judge) Marlin Applewick, came up with the tacky idea to award members with Tasmanian Devil geegaws whenever one of us made a fiery floor speech. All Democrats could do was talk because we didn't have enough votes to pass anything, and we had no allies across the aisle.

The new Republican majority was ideologically extremely conservative. My liberal bubble burst early in a hearing before the Natural Resources Committee, when Republican Representative Val Stevens argued that requiring life jackets for children in boats was a violation of parental rights. What an eye-opening time! And, sadly, a precursor of things to come.

Upon my appointment for the sixty-day legislative session, I'd had to scramble. I was able to negotiate unpaid leave from my job, with a right to return after the session. I had a husband who was lukewarm to the idea of his wife being a politician. Our three kids didn't seem to care one way or the other but wanted their mom when they needed her. It was the same, harried juggling act that working moms do all over our country. Somehow we managed, but looking back, I'm not quite sure how.

After that first session, I realized that to keep my seat I had to figure out how to run a campaign. There were no training programs or support systems for women at the time. The spectacular victories of the Year of the Woman made headlines in 1992, but those newly elected women, such as U.S. Senator Patty Murray, had their hands full with their own milestones to meet and cross. EMILY's List (Early Money Is Like Yeast), a political action committee supporting women candidates that focused on federal races, wasn't active in state legislative races. Back then, my legislative district was known as a swing district—it had a long Republican history and a few recent Democratic wins but was still considered a toss-up.

I did have a wonderful seatmate who was generous with her time and knowledge. Representative Julia Patterson helped me find many local resources and supporters I would have never stumbled across in my journey.

She had been one of the organizers behind the cityhood referendum that created the City of SeaTac, and when she decided to run for a seat in the legislature, I supported her campaign. She remembered my support; in return, she showed me where to put yard signs, introduced me to local officials I had never met, and even shared her campaign's graphic artist to help design my campaign literature.

This was during the days before a professional political consultant class was available for most legislative races, so we had to do everything ourselves. It was quite the learning experience!

I had never in my life gone doorbelling, except as a Girl Scout selling cookies back in Iowa.

Julia showed me how. It isn't rocket science. But it was all new to me, and I had to learn fast.

KEY TAKEAWAYS

- Ignorance may be bliss, but experience and knowledge create power to make change.
- You have to believe in yourself and your values to take on the risk to run for election.
- Juggling jobs and career, family life, and legislative duties is a challenge but it can be managed.
- Seek out and appreciate incumbents who mentor and help new legislators

NOTES

1. Chicago humorist Finley Peter Dunne wrote in a 1902 newspaper column: "Th' *newspaper* does ivrything f'r us. It runs th' polis foorce an' th' banks, commands th' milishy, conthrols th' ligislachure, baptizes th' young, marries th' foolish, comforts th' afflicted, afflicts th' comfortable, buries th' dead an' roasts thim aftherward." Reinhold Niebuhr, the liberal theologian, also used the quote in his essays.

2. "On this day, August 5, 1981, President Reagan fires 11,000 air traffic controllers," www. Politico.com/story/2008/08/reagan-fires-11,000-striking-air-traffic.

3. Maureen Dowd, "Vengeful Glee (and Sweetness) At Gingrich's Victory Party," *New York Times*, November 9, 1994.

CHAPTER 2

Early Lessons

"Once you stop learning, you start dying."
—Albert Einstein

Everything seems possible when you win your first legislative race. You know you can change your world for the better through legislative action. But it isn't easy. It pays to keep your eye on the prize as long as you don't become so repetitive that people tune you out.

I've found two fundamental traits essential: core values and persistence. Every state legislature in the United States is distinct, with different traditions, procedures, committees, power brokers and breakers.

"There are many rules and norms in the legislature," Senator T'wina Nobles quickly discovered. "What I have learned in my short time as a state senator is that many of these rules and norms are not written. You simply have to experience it."

Along the way, it soon becomes apparent that some elements of legislative success are universal.

You need to build a bridge to unlikely supporters—to figure out a way to get them to say "yes" instead of "no." "No" comes easy. "Yes" takes real effort, and then some. Take the time to have coffee and a conversation with all the members on all your committees and beyond.

You need allies—not just in the other chamber but across the aisle and outside the doors of the legislature.

You need to hard-count your votes and then figure out how to get some more for a solid count you can depend on.

You need a persuasive argument for why change is necessary—now—and not merely something you desire.

Jeff Holy, today a Republican state senator, had been a delegate for the Washington Council of Police and Sheriffs, lobbying in Olympia on their behalf for several years, and his civil law practice had morphed into a government affairs practice. "By the end of 2011," he said, "I really thought that I knew what the legislature was all about."

Upon winning election to the state House of Representatives in 2013, Holy quickly realized how mistaken he was. "It took only one day," he said, "for me to realize that I had essentially stepped through the looking glass and didn't have any real idea how the dynamics, interpersonal relationships and decision-making processes happened in the legislature."

Claire Wilson, a Democrat, had a similar experience upon her election to the Senate.

"After over twenty-five years of working in schools, government, and on school boards, I was more prepared than most to enter the legislature—and I still spent much of my first two years figuring out how it all works."

When I joined the House Democratic Caucus in 1995, Democrats were in the minority. That was a gift because I had the luxury of being able to learn how things worked without the expectation of actually passing a bill.

Even at that, I think I must be a very slow learner because it took me three years to get my first bill passed into law. But it was a "good little bill"—parlance for legislation so uncontroversial that no one would reasonably oppose it—that eliminated the requirement for all home buyers to purchase PMI (private mortgage insurance), a bill that could save homeowners hundreds of dollars a year in unnecessary insurance.[1] Even Republicans voted for it, and I needed their votes since the Democrats were still in the minority.

That was my first lesson: you need to build bridges to get unlikely supporters to say "maybe" or even "yes."

Because I had been appointed to fill a vacancy, I had no opportunity to request committee assignments; I just took what I was given. One was the Financial Institutions Committee. I had no background or expertise in banking, insurance regulations, or other financial issues. Nevertheless, as an enthusiastic but naive novice, I happily dug into the entrails of such arcane matters as private mortgage insurance and insurance guaranty funds. That fall, my campaign committee began receiving checks from sundry banks and financial firms, without my even asking for their donations! I accepted the donations and reminded myself of Willie Sutton's retort when asked why he robbed banks: "Because that's where the money is."

House Leadership was watching out for me—an untested freshman in a district that wasn't safe for Democrats[2]—by giving me a spot on the money committee and a head start on fundraising. I didn't realize at the time what they had done for me, and I don't think I ever thanked them. The donations were useful, but I knew in hindsight that my longtime friends, allies, and supporters were the real reason I was able to win that first election.

That campaign taught me my second lesson: you need all kinds of allies supporting you both inside and outside the doors of the legislature, and some will surprise you.

That first campaign was hard, although I had lots of local volunteers who helped me in so many ways. I put together a kitchen cabinet of local folks who could organize different campaign duties and help stuff envelopes, pound in yard signs, and make telephone calls back when those tasks were the nuts and bolts of a campaign. I spent nearly every day (except Fridays, when people often aren't home) from May through mid-October knocking on doors in different neighborhood precincts from 3:00 to 7:00 p.m. and on weekends from 10:00 a.m. to 6:00 p.m., except for Seahawks' Sunday football games when voters really got annoyed at answering a doorbell during the game. Sometimes one of my kids would come along and help, but mostly they preferred not to. Could I blame them? I was grateful for whatever help they gave.

As an appointed incumbent, I had a slight advantage, but my Republican opponent had run before and had more experience. I won the election, but it was a slim victory.[3]

I remember walking out on the driveway and looking up at the stars that night, wondering what in the world I was getting myself into. My husband was traveling on another one of his freelance jobs, and the kids were all in bed. I wondered where I was going to end up. I had taken leave from my day job for two months of full time campaigning, but after the election I had to get back to work until the legislative session convened in January of 1995.

That election taught me my third lesson: know how many votes you need to win, and then go after more votes to give you solid numbers you can count on. In the legislature, the same vote-count discipline is essential for your bills to pass.

When you first enter the legislature, the ceremonial pomp and circumstance—the grand marble hallways and historic building, not to mention all the other elected officials—can intimidate you or put you in awe of what you have accomplished to get there. But reality can intrude quickly.

After attending a number of fancy formals, festivities, and receptions in Olympia, Senator Jeff Holy asked his wife, Cindy, what she thought of it all. "It reminds me of *The Wizard of Oz*," she replied, "where Dorothy pulls back the curtain and finds that there is no wizard—only a guy from Kansas—and these legislators are all people from Kansas."

Still, it's important not to let the initial awe wear off. It can inspire you when you're in a tough spot, and it can motivate you to achieve your goals.

Newly elected women, and especially women of color, are often not recognized or treated with the same respect as the male members. It's important to step forward and introduce yourself, to assert your identity to both staff and lobbyists. It takes considerably more effort than is required of male lawmakers, but a strong impression is necessary to establish yourself as a person and member to be recognized and respected. I know of a recently elected woman of color who was challenged by security when she entered the Senate chamber. The security guard didn't recognize her as a senator and apparently assumed a person of color had no business there. I can vouch for the fact that that would never have happened to a white male or female member.

As a freshman, first-term legislator, you will have some space to make mistakes and perhaps receive gifts of bills that others have developed and worked on that you can carry across the finish line. (After your first reelection, the gifts will end.) Your first couple of years are an opportunity for learning and achieving some wins for your district and identifying your priorities. It's also your opportunity as a new member to establish your credibility and reliability. Unfortunately, it's still a reality that women and people of color often have to reach a higher bar to establish themselves.

That brings me to lesson four: learn how best to make a persuasive case to your colleagues that your proposal is necessary.

To make significant change takes time, but it also demands a compelling argument that can move members to "yes"—or at least from "no" to "maybe." Persuasion is the art of getting people to understand that what you seek is also in their best interest.

If you can show how your approach will work and help their constituents, that helps. Clear communication is vital. Focus first on members who are open to you and your concerns. Don't waste time on ideologues. Identify which of your colleagues is what you might call a swing voter. And if someone wants a favor in return, consider the possibility of reciprocity. If the exchange is reasonable, you might be able to strike a good deal.

As a candidate, you successfully persuaded voters to elect you. As a lawmaker, you will need to use that gift of persuasion to win support for your bill, or your amendment, or your budget item. Have a ready answer to the question: Why is this necessary, and why is it needed now? Ask yourself first so you will know the answer before you are asked.

KEY TAKEAWAYS

- You can never have too many votes or too much support. Enough is not enough.

- Treat your first session as a learning experience and remember your lessons.

- Establish a reputation for credibility and reliability early, and build on it.

- Introduce yourself to staff, lobbyists, and security staff so they will know you and remember who you are.

NOTES

1. 199–98: HB 2611, Regulating Mortgage Insurance, signed into law, April 1, 1998.

2. My 33rd legislative district was considered a swing district for good reason. I eked out a victory with just 52.45 percent of the vote in 1996 to Republican Jim McCune's 47.55 percent. Two years later, McCune ran again and won in the 33rd District with 50.59 percent of the votes against appointed incumbent Rod Blalock, a heartbreaking 49.41 percent loss. Later, McCune moved to the 2nd District in Pierce County, where he won a House seat again and served four years. In 2020 he ran for the 2nd LD Senate seat and won.

3. My opponent Jim McCune subsequently moved to a new district and ran again. He won a seat and now serves across the aisle from me in the Senate.

CHAPTER 3

What is Your Legislative Path?

"The freshman legislator's critical act or oversight is to make the correct decisions early as to what he or she wishes to specialize in."
—State Senator George W. Scott[1]

Newly elected lawmakers can easily be overwhelmed by all the new information and decisions awaiting them. It's often called a "water hose" of things to learn. But don't drown or choke on it. Think ahead. One of the first things each newly elected lawmaker should consider is which path forward to pursue. Most legislative chambers have three different tracks:

1 **Policy.** Many lawmakers focus on issues, often the issues that prompted them to run for office in the first place. Policy is formed in the standing committees organized around policies such as health care, labor, education, environment, economic development, and so on. Generally, the committee chair sets the agenda for which bills will be heard, which bills will be moved forward, which bills will be amended, and which bills will die. Some states, such as Colorado, observe a process where all bills must be heard and voted on in committee, but even these states have ways to kill bills using other options.

2 **Budget.** Many policy committee chairs also serve on the main budget committee so they can shepherd the funding for the issues they prioritize. Budgets are huge and complicated. Indeed, the budget bill is often considered the most important bill of the entire session. A seat on the budget committee also gives you a window to the breadth by which state legislation impacts the specific communities in your district. Digging into the details of the budget and becoming expert in a specific area will increase your influence for change.

3 **Leadership.** Becoming Speaker of the House or Majority Leader or Minority Leader of the Senate, or part of the team of leadership insiders who shape the session, has the whiff and sometimes whip of power politics.

(Different states may use different leadership titles but the essence of the roles is similar.) The leverage that comes with a leadership position can make it much easier to accomplish goals aligned with your values—and can similarly be employed to prevent bad things as well.

After every election, each caucus in the legislature undertakes a reorganization to consider everyone's roles. Newly elected members must be integrated and departing members must be replaced. At the same time, an incumbent member might seek a larger role or position in a fresh policy area. That means positions on House (or Assembly) and Senate committees will need to be filled and often rearranged.

Each chamber is organized around party caucuses (except in Nebraska, where the legislature has only one chamber). Leaders for each caucus—in the House or Assembly it's the Speaker and Minority Leader, and in the Senate it's the Majority Leader and Minority Leader—are elected along with the members the leader wants on the leadership team.[2] Leaders and potential leaders will try to persuade other members to enlist their support and votes. These internal elections take place after the November general election and before the holidays, so newly-elected lawmakers are sometimes surprised by the quick shift to political positioning so quickly after the election.[3]

Positions such as Floor Leader, Whip, Caucus Chair, and Assistant Floor Leader can be appointed or elected as a slate. Women, and especially women of color, will need to assert themselves and talk to the caucus leader if they want to serve on the leadership team. Obviously, you have a better chance of winning a spot on the leadership team if you supported the leader in the reorganization election. If you backed a losing candidate, reach out to the winner as soon as you can to open the lines of communication. Be alert, and keep your eyes and ears open.

New members are often picked to work as an Assistant Whip, which is a great way to get to know all the members of your caucus. It's also an opportunity to see whether you like the leadership track or prefer a policy or budget track. As newly elected Senator Claire Wilson told me, "I had no clue what a Whip was" when she was assigned the Assistant Whip position.[4] She quickly learned and became adept at tracking members' votes on important bills working their way to the floor.

There are no formal job descriptions for these positions, but they operate pretty much like this:

• The Whip and Assistant Whip count the votes of caucus members on controversial bills. They must have the trust of their colleagues and keep their vote counts confidential, reporting only to the leadership of the caucus.

- The Floor Leader and Assistant Floor Leader usually assign bills that are introduced to a respective standing policy or fiscal committee, although in some states this duty falls to the Senate President or Speaker. Sometimes the choices are obvious, as when a bill on prescription drugs is assigned to the Health Care Committee, but sometimes not so obvious. Should a bill to require a simple majority on school levies, for instance, go to the Education Committee or to the Local Government Committee? The choice might be driven by logic, but just as often it can be influenced by politics and power. Is a keenly-watched bill on water quality more likely to be supported by the committee overseeing water rights or the committee overseeing environmental health? Knowing which lawmakers sit on those committees and their track records on water issues can mean the difference between a welcome reception or a place for the bill to die. Sometimes the sponsor of a bill might insist the bill be assigned to a committee she chairs, even if that committee is not the most obvious match, simply because her role as chair gives her more power over the fate of the bill. During floor action, the Floor Leader keeps track of all bills in the process and creates floor calendars tracking when each bill that has been pulled to the floor will come up for an actual vote. The Floor Leader also makes procedural motions and must master the parliamentary knowledge and skills necessary to employ the rules and motions of the House or Senate (Reeds Rules, Mason's Manual, Jefferson's Manual, Robert's Rules). We'll talk more about rules in Chapter 19, "You Can Call Me Madam President."

- The Caucus Chair and Assistant Chair call and run the caucus meetings—we'll talk about caucus meetings in more detail in Chapter 6, "Behind Closed Doors"—but for now let's just say that it's easy for passionate or opinionated members to get into heated discussions on controversial issues, making it important to have a firm and savvy hand managing the caucus meetings. The Caucus Chair may also organize or host social events as a team building exercise.

- Caucus leaders, Speakers, Senate Presidents, Majority Leaders, and Minority Leaders all bring strong personalities and their own styles. Some are very controlling; some are more inclusive.

Internal politics is rife in caucus, but leadership isn't often contested. When it is, it can become unpleasant, but not always. The 2019 leadership election in the Washington House of Representatives was a first—the three representatives running for the open Speaker's seat were all women. After Washington state's first-ever female Speaker of the House was sworn in for the 2020 session, the two candidates who lost received plum committee positions.

Prior to each legislative session, the leaders appoint members to their Committee on Committees, a farcical sounding but extremely powerful group that determines which members are assigned to each of the various policy and budget committees. New members don't usually serve on this committee, but they need to know who does. In some states there is no Committee on Committees; instead, caucus leadership chooses all committee assignments.

As always, it is vital for new members to reach out to the members on the Committee on Committees and be ready to have a persuasive conversation about why you should be appointed to the committees you want. For women especially, this is the beginning of an endless balancing act of asserting yourself without becoming "annoying" or "too aggressive." Unless you already have close relationships with members on the Committee on Committees, it is important to let them know your interests and strengths. As a new member, first impressions can advance or slow your progress.

I was blind to the nuances of these choices when I took office. I didn't even realize what a privileged appointment it was to be on the Committee of Committees until I got a seat at that table. Voting on who should be the chair of a key committee and who should be on that committee is an exercise in both judgment and power. Some people use it to reward friends and punish opponents, but my experience has been that most consider the choices from all angles.

In my first few years, I asked to be on the Education Committee. My kids were still all in public school, and I felt I had a ringside view of the educational needs and challenges. I also asked to stay on the Financial Institutions Committee because I realized that future fundraising would be much easier if I kept that seat. With my job in organized labor, leadership was wary of appointing me to sit on the Labor and Economic Development Committee. That was disappointing but, as a consolation, I was appointed to the powerful Appropriations Committee. Little did I know then the importance of the budget committees. But with the incredibly skilled leadership of the legendary Appropriations Committee chair, Representative Helen Sommers, I received what amounted to a graduate course in budget making.

Helen Sommers is the only woman to have a building on the Washington State Capital Campus named after her. First elected in 1972, she served thirty-six years. Sommers was the no-nonsense chair of the House Appropriations Committee for many years, and she always made sure reproductive health care was protected and funded. As an impenetrable bulwark in defense of public pensions, she refused to allow the underfunding of pensions, an unsound policy that led to dangerous pension insolvency in other states. Sommers insisted on generous funding to higher education, especially her alma mater, the University of Washington. She was short in stature but a towering presence. As her friend Representative Eileen Cody observed, "She was a little thing with a lot of power."[5] She also recruited many women to run for the legislature, including me.

Most state budgets spend more on health care and education than any other areas. Corrections, human services, environment, and everything else account for around 20 percent. (However, many environmental and natural resources projects are primarily funded in the capital construction budgets.) Coincidentally, education and health care are two go-to policy committees for many newly elected women legislators. But those same new women members must ask for, want, and work for appointment to one of their chamber's fiscal committees.

New members in the Washington State Senate often wind up assigned to the Transportation Committee as their first fiscal committee. That was also my assignment when I first got into the Senate, and it seemed to me we spent most of the time approving new license plate designs. Transportation dollars typically rely on license fees and the gas tax, which is a dwindling source of revenue in this age of higher mile-per-gallon vehicles, electric and hybrid engines, and reduced travel. To actually build new capacity, transportation bonds must be sold. Bonds are a debt instrument and in most states require the approval of 60 percent of the legislature to pass. With slim party majorities, bipartisan support is necessary to approve bonds, whether for transportation projects or capital (infrastructure) construction.

Bipartisan support rarely reaches 60 percent for the big money of the Operating Budget, which funds the ongoing operation of the vast majority of public services, from K–12 education and colleges, to prisons and health care, and the overall social safety net.

In Washington state, the big-money Operating Budget is written by the Ways and Means Committee in the Senate and by the Finance and Appropriations committees in the House. The biennial two-year budget is often described as the most important bill of the session—though it is filled with numbers, it is actually the most meaningful policy document because its allocations dictate which services are considered the most important. It is also a vehicle many members use to further their personal goals, whether it's finding funding for a favorite nonprofit program or resources for a district project. Close reading is required.

"Where there's money, there's also frequently mischief," U.S. House Speaker Nancy Pelosi warned in April of 2020 when creating a special congressional panel focused on rooting out waste and fraud in the Trump Administration's pandemic response.[6] Pelosi knew the massive response was urgently needed but that it was also a prime opening for opportunists to steer funds to special interests. As reporters often advise, "Follow the money."

The Washington State House has three separate fiscal committees—Capital Budget, Appropriations, and Finance. Finance is the committee that passes tax bills and projected revenue is calculated into the House budget. The Appropriations Committee appropriates the expected revenues for the entire state. The Capital Budget Committee is the happiest fiscal committee to be on because its funds build schools, affordable housing, water projects, college campuses, community recreation centers, parks, cultural, and nonprofit projects. What's not to love? One of my favorite jobs ever was when I was the Democratic lead on the Capital Budget Committee, which is part of the Ways and Means Committee work in the Senate. We were in the minority at the time, which is not a pleasant place to be, but I still enjoyed my work because the Capitol Budget had such a positive focus.

Public education, including higher education, accounts for nearly 60 percent of the Washington state general Operating Budget. Health care accounts for another 20–25 percent of the budget. Those two huge chunks of spending are heavily lobbied, and all bills passed by the Education or Health Care committees that cost money (and most do) need to also pass the fiscal committee to be included in the budget and actually go into effect.

One of the least understood hurdles for all new members is the Operating Budget, and many women lawmakers seem to avoid the committees that write that budget. Perhaps it's a vestige of an "I'm not good at math" mindset. But a seat on that committee provides a broad overall view of the key functions of the entire state government and also gives you the influence to change funding in areas you think should be adjusted.

The general budget is an amazingly complex, almost living organism, with nooks and crannies that only the professional committee staff fully understand. I think of it as an onion—year after year, another layer will be revealed if you peel it.

Capital budget negotiations in 2015 with Senator Mark Mullet, a moderate Democrat from King County suburbs. We are going point by point over some language.

Serving on the main fiscal committee is hard work. It takes hours and hours of hearings and meetings, sometimes marathon in duration, requiring multiple twelve-hour sessions as budget deadlines near; but it's worth it. The Ways and Means Committee and Appropriations Committee are important, powerful committees.

It isn't easy to get appointed to them, but I strongly recommend expressing your interest to leadership and asking Committee on Committees members for an appointment. If you want to succeed in making real change, you need more than beautiful policy—you must manage to get the money in the budget to successfully implement it.

KEY TAKEAWAYS

- Choose your path forward; don't just allow others to put you in your place.
- Specialize early in a policy or budget area where you want to make change.

- Stretch yourself to learn about the most important bill in any legislative session: the General Fund Budget (also called the Operating Budget).
- Focus your attention on what you are most passionate about in both policy and budget.
- Follow the money.

NOTES

1. George W. Scott, *A Majority of One: Legislative Life* (Seattle: Civitas Press, 2002), 27.

2. States use different leadership titles. In states with a House (also called an Assembly in some states), the top leader of that chamber is the Speaker—except in North Dakota, where the Majority Leader is the top position. Senate President is the top Senate position in twenty-four states. In Washington, Wisconsin, Minnesota, Iowa, North Dakota, Virginia, and Nevada, the top Senate position is Majority Leader. In Alabama, Texas, Georgia, Tennessee, and Mississippi, the Lieutenant Governor plays a larger role and serves as Senate Leader. In the other twelve states, the top leader is the Senate President Pro Tempore. In Nebraska, it's the Speaker of the Senate. Also, four states—Texas, Mississippi, Nebraska, and Louisiana—do not recognize minority leaders.

3. National Conference of State Legislators, "Be More Effective," *Mastering the Rules*, podcast, https://www.ncsl.org/research/about-state-legislatures/podcasts-how-to-be-an-effective-legislator.aspx.

4. Senator Claire Wilson was elected in 2018 to the Washington State Senate, 30th Legislative District, and appointed Assistant Whip in the 2019–2020 sessions.

5. Joseph O'Sullivan, "Rep. Helen Sommers Dies: She Served in State House for 35 Years," *Seattle Times*, March 7, 2017.

6. Erica Werner, and Paul Kane, "Pelosi announces new select committee to oversee coronavirus response, setting up clash with Trump over $2 trillion law," *The Washington Post*, April 2, 2020.

CHAPTER 4

Making Sausage

"You do what you can and then you do some more."
—Hazel Wolf[1]

Any new arrival to the legislature will quickly and often hear legislation compared to the process of making sausage. It borders on cliché, but it's apt, nevertheless.

The recipe for sausage is simple, but the making of sausage is rather ugly. You put several pounds of pork meat and fat through a coarse grind, then add lots of herbs and spices, often including some sage, and a bit of sherry to bind it. Then you do a fine grind of all the ingredients. You can fry it up in patties or go to the effort of stuffing it into pork casings. Most of us would prefer to get our sausage premade at a supermarket or butcher shop. The flavor of a well-made link surpasses the sum of its parts. Good sausage is all about balance, between salt and savory, meat and fat, and spices and herbs. Beyond the basic recipe, your ingredient list is limited only by your imagination.

Comparing sausage making to lawmaking makes for a fitting analogy. Like sausage, legislation is limited only by your imagination and comes in all kinds of flavors and packaging. But please consider a little "sage advice"—as a freshman, keep it simple and have a clear message.

The mere act of reading a bill is often confusing. References to state legal code numbers in the underlying law will sound arcane unless you are a lawyer, and the vast majority of lawmakers are not. To the typical newly elected legislator, bill language can be incomprehensible. The easiest route to get a general idea about a bill is to read the bill report or summary, which is written in terms nearer to plain English. But the clarity of the report will vary with the expertise of its author, and most staff won't write a bill report until a bill is formally scheduled for a hearing. Many bills don't even get that far.

If you don't understand a bill that you are interested in or that your committee will be hearing, ask one of the professionals either on the committee staff or caucus staff to discuss it with you—and don't be embarrassed to admit you don't understand something. The language of legislation frequently needs a translator, and a bill's ramifications and impact may go well beyond what you originally thought. That's one of the purposes of committee hearings: to tease out and discover some of the hidden or underlying ramifications of complex legislative proposals.

The legislative journey can include many twists and turns, as a bill that starts out as one thing can turn into another and then another as it winds its way through the process. In some chambers, a bill's title cannot be amended, and any additional or amended language must fit within the scope of the title. But in other chambers, the bill title can be changed, and the bill language can be amended to match the new title, often radically. It gets tricky sometimes.

Once your bill has been drafted, be sure to read the damn thing. And if it is amended, either by you or by someone else, scrutinize the amended language carefully. Standard protocol is to inform the prime sponsor of a bill of any proposed amendments. A surprise amendment is usually hostile to the bill's purpose, so be on guard for such surprises. I had a colleague who was highly successful at amending bills to her liking simply by relying on other lawmakers' disinclination to read bills.

Bills often begin with an intent section to emphasize the purpose of the bill. It isn't required, is not necessary, and has no real force of law, but it can be helpful to communicate your goals.

The definition section in a bill can be routine or clever, and watch out for the clever ones. Depending on who drafted the bill, the language may be clear or it may be intentionally cryptic. The more convoluted the language, the more likely it contains some surprises. Most bills are a few pages long. Some bills, including budget bills, run hundreds of pages. During a particularly heated floor fight some years back, our caucus delayed a vote on a bill that had been pulled unexpectedly to the floor by making the parliamentary motion to have the bill formally read, word for word.[2] It was the biennial budget bill and took hours to read, providing the caucus precious time to draft numerous amendments to the bill. Computer search functions can also ease your task.

In the kitchen, sausage is often made by following a familiar, predictable recipe. In the legislature, there are a lot of cooks who may want to tweak your recipe as your bill moves through the process. Keep an eye on every step to make sure what comes out in the end is what you intended.

KEY TAKEAWAYS

- Read your own bills.

- If you don't understand something in a bill, ask for an explanation.

- Be wary of convoluted language, unusual definitions, or surprise amendments.

- No bill is perfect or ends up in law exactly as it started.

NOTES

1. Hazel Wolf (March 10, 1898–January 19, 2000) was a Seattle-based feminist, union organizer, civil rights activist, and environmentalist.

2. In the 2012 session, with a slim majority, three Senate Democrats (Tim Sheldon, Jim Kastama, and Rodney Tom) joined with Republicans to take over the floor and pass a Republican budget. A demand motion was made by Floor Leader Senator Tracey Eide. A demand motion only requires one senator with no supporting votes. Once made, it cannot be stopped unless the demand is withdrawn by the person who makes the motion (Rule 64 and Rule 65). However, under Reeds Rule 212, a member may not abuse the rules of the body in order to obstruct public business. Under Reeds Rule 49, no member may make use of a parliamentary procedure to impede unreasonably the action of the assembly. The President of the Senate shall rule on the motion.

CHAPTER 5

From Rhetoric to Reality

"You campaign in poetry, you govern in prose."
—Governor Mario Cuomo

Before your first legislative session begins, a reckoning takes place for many newly elected members. How do you transform your campaign rhetoric into legislation that will actually pass and make a difference for your constituents? It's a tall order.

Legislative sessions are usually intense and short, so any head start you can get is well worth the effort. Begin as soon as you know what committees you will be serving on. Find out who else is on those committees and research whether you might have some common interests. Be sure and introduce yourself to the committee chair and share what interests you would like to work on with her. She can help open many doors for you, including connecting you with the right staff people.

Nearly all legislatures have professional nonpartisan committee staff who can help. Some legislatures have partisan caucus staff who can help. Some have personal staff hired to help during a session. I think one of the big reasons the Washington State Legislature leads the way on so many issues is because we have all three.

Having a professional legislative staff also helps to balance the power of the executive branch. Before full-time professional legislative staffs were provided, the governor was totally in charge and dominated state policies, according to Representative Helen Sommers. First elected in 1973, she recalled that "the professional, non-partisan committee staff…the administrative staff and also partisan caucus staff…gave the legislature more equal footing."[1]

Washington has a nonpartisan staff of highly skilled professionals and lawyers who can help legislators write bills and advise them on potential options. Second, we are blessed with a highly skilled caucus staff with considerable expertise in issue areas—in many states there are fewer caucus staff or even no caucus staff. Third, we have personally hired office staff, an option unavailable in a number of states. This allows legislators to apply a team-effort approach to their work that also builds institutional knowledge.

On high-profile issues, you will likely know and meet with lots of advocates on both sides. Each will want to help shape the issue and amend any legislative language that's offered. Advocates can be very helpful, but they all bring their own biases and, as a legislator, it's now your job to develop your own views and make your own decisions. Advocates are essential to hear from and work with because no one person knows it all, and new information is useful. But legislators should not and cannot simply be mouthpieces. That's the job of lobbyists.

So here are some first steps:

1 Depending on which committees you've been assigned to, be sure and connect with the committee chair to discuss your ideas and goals. The chair may well have some suggestions, and it is wise to hear them. It's best if the chair and you are from the same political party. But if not, it is especially important to meet with and talk with your chair if you want your bill proposal to at least receive a public hearing in her committee.

2 Ask committee staff or caucus staff to draft an initial bill to reflect your ideas and goals. They will ask you a lot of questions to clarify your thinking. These questions are also sometimes soft suggestions of what may actually work, both legally and legislatively.

3 Read the first draft. Ask questions, make edits, and request changes that seem needed.

4 Run your bill idea past someone in the other chamber whom you know might be able to work on it from her side of the rotunda, including seatmates from your legislative district if they are on the same page as you.

5 Meet with advocates and discuss the draft. Include staff in the meetings so they can hear and understand the dynamics of the differing viewpoints. You might, or might not, want to share the actual draft language; staff may be able to help you decide what's best based on past experience with the issue and those affected by it.

6 You may also want to meet with potential opponents to test the parameters of how open they are to negotiation. This can be helpful or hurtful, so consider this step carefully, and be cautious about which information you share.

7 After discussing options with staff, update the draft to reflect any advocates' suggestions that you think make sense. You can easily go through five or six drafts of a bill on a complex issue before you send it off to the code reviser's office to be translated into exacting legal language so that it reads as a law. As with the initial draft, meet again with advocates to discuss the updated draft. And again include staff in the meetings and consult with them on whether to share the actual draft language.

Capital budget floor negotiations, 2015: Sometimes things go well, sometimes not so well in floor negotiations. In these photos I am working to get to "yes" with Republican Senators.

All this preparation will help move your bill through the arduous legislative process. It's a long haul with many steps along the way to the governor's desk to be signed into law.

Once your bill comes back from the code reviser, it will have a cover sheet for signatures. The first signature will be yours as the bill's prime sponsor. Lawmakers often want to document support for their bill by gathering other legislators' signatures on the cover sheet as cosponsors. It can also be useful to collect signatures from a few members on the other side of the aisle if you want to indicate bipartisan support. (Electronic signatures are now options instead of physical cover sheets.) Of course, this method doesn't apply for hot-button partisan bills that are often known as "message bills"—not likely to pass, these bills are introduced to bring attention to a position, politician, or issue. In any case, it is helpful to include a short memo describing the bill for members whom you ask to sign on as cosponsors.

After you sign your bill on the top line and gather other signatures as needed, it's time to "drop your bill in the Hopper," which is an old-fashioned term from legislatures long ago.[2] It means depositing it in the House Speaker's or Secretary of the Senate's box for new bills. Following the COVID-19 pandemic, bills can now be dropped in an electronic "hopper" as well. Once your bill is dropped, it will be assigned a bill number and becomes a public document. You might also want to notify colleagues of your bill number and ask them to sign on after it is published in the Introductions of Bills sheet (if your chamber rules allow that). Once the bill is introduced, suddenly you will have lobbyists contacting you to talk about their concerns. This all happens in the first week or two of the session. It is hectic and confusing.

Here's what comes next:

1 Request a public hearing for your bill from the chair of whatever committee the bill is assigned to. This is usually a formal request in writing by letter or email because committee chairs are too busy managing the bills to make time for a personal meeting. But if you have established a friendship with the chair, a personal request works even better.

2 Once the bill is scheduled for a public hearing, don't forget to contact advocates who can come or who can bring people to come to the committee to testify in support. (The saddest events are when a member proposes a bill and no one supports it in the hearing.) One or two strong personal testimonies will often outweigh the typical lobbyist's testimony.

3 After the public hearing, if opposition testimony was weak or nonexistent, ask the chair to move your bill to executive action as soon as possible for a vote to pass out of committee. If there was a lot of opposition, you will have need to address their concerns or reach an agreement with the members of the committee that your bill is a work in progress—this implies you are continuing to negotiate its terms but want to get the bill moving through the lengthy legislative process. Try to get it voted on and passed out of the policy committee as soon as you can, especially if it has a fiscal note or will cost money, because if it does, the bill will also need to go before the budget committee where the bill must again be scheduled for a hearing and moved to executive session for a vote before it can be sent to the Rules Committee. The Rules Committee is the last stop before a bill can be brought to the floor of the Senate or House for a vote of the full chamber, except in the few states where bills automatically go from the policy committee to the floor. Leadership controls the Rules Committee to ensure that priority bills get to the floor and to prevent unwelcome bills from making it to the floor. As a freshman member, your caucus's leadership should help you move your bill along. One tip: swift action in committee can mean the difference between your bill's ultimate passage

or failure; legislation that lingers in committee faces increasingly stiff competition and dwindling time to be acted on as legislative deadlines get closer.

4 Now that your bill has made it through the committee process, you face a new set of realities: the floor. Floor action has its own dynamic, and each one is managed by the leadership team, including the Floor Leader, the Whips, and the Speaker or Majority Leader. But first your bill will be presented in caucus, usually by the chair or, if you are in the minority, by the ranking minority member of the committee that heard your bill. Caucus meetings are private conversations about bills between members of the same party, managed by the Caucus Chair. What is said in caucus is supposed to stay in caucus so that lawmakers feel free to discuss any concerns openly and candidly. After a robust debate on a bill, the Whip and Assistant Whip will do a vote count of legislators. If the caucus discussion is calm, with apparent consensus, the bill will likely move forward. But if the vote count reveals opposition or inadequate support, the bill will not be put on the floor calendar to get a floor vote. It will simply die (although it could be resurrected sometime in the future, perhaps in a new form). If your bill is passed off the floor, it is sent to the opposite chamber, and there the process starts all over again, but with less time.

5 If you are in the minority party, you are at the mercy of the majority party, and you will have to negotiate or ingratiate yourself across the aisle to get your bill to the floor calendar for a floor vote.

6 It's often said that killing a bill is one of the easier things to do in a session and, indeed, many lobbyists are hired for just that job. With all the steps and hurdles built into the process, it's amazing how many bills actually get passed into law. New legislators usually get a helping hand for the first couple of years, but there is no school for the process—it comes down to on-the-job training and, after a couple of years, you are on your own. Mentors and personal relationships are two of the ways to help you become an effective legislator who can effectively shepherd bills through and who can help others get their bills moving too.

One last tip: whether it involves your bill or someone else's, when your committee is hearing testimony on a bill, be a good host and listener. Although it's sometimes necessary to question a testifier to provide clarity, it's poor form to challenge or attack a testifier simply because you disagree with their view. Of course, professional lobbyists who have created obstacles for important bills

A view of the chamber podium in 2018 as the vote is counted by the attorneys for each caucus during a procedural call for a "division," a standing vote count. I am presiding for this vote count, which is often contentious and sometimes fractious.

can take the heat of a grilling, but committee testimony is generally a time to hear the public's concerns, not to argue the merits of their testimony or the related legislation. When a committee chair or member berates or bullies someone who is testifying, it sends two terrible messages—first, that the lawmaker is unwilling to entertain a differing viewpoint or information and, second, that the public's input is not welcome. Anyone who has signed on to serve as a legislator has accepted the responsibility to do "the people's work" in "the people's house"; the people should always be welcome and treated with courtesy and respect (unless they themselves exhibit inappropriate behavior).

KEY TAKEAWAYS

- Get to know the chairs of the committees you are appointed to. Introduce yourself and give them an idea about the bill(s) you want to introduce.

- Create a team to support your bill, taking advice and assistance from your personal staff, caucus staff, and committee professionals.

- Talk to your colleagues about your bill and ask them to cosponsor it as a show of support before you formally introduce it and also after it is introduced.

- Work with the advocates for your bill, and make sure they will support it in meetings and in committee hearings.

NOTES

1. Helen Sommers, An Oral History, Washington State Archives, 1969–70, page 31.

2. "Stories from the People's House": "The term hopper refers to the entry bin of a grain machine and represents the initial phase of a bill's journey…much like grain when processed into flour." https://history.house.gov/BLOG2014/August8-4-The_Hopper.

CHAPTER 6

Behind Closed Doors

"Illegitimi non carborundum."
—Personal motto of General Joseph Stilwell (a mock Latin aphorism often translated
as, "Don't let the bastards grind you down.")

During the days when the legislature is scheduled for floor action, when members will vote on bills that have made it to the floor calendar, a seemingly endless stream of hours is spent behind the heavy oak doors of the party caucus rooms. Members of each party assemble in their caucus rooms for confidential discussions, debates, descriptions, and reports. The main business is caucusing on bills or reviewing a list of bills on the Second Reading Calendar that may be brought to the floor for a vote. (Second reading means they are available for floor action or amendment.)

Each chamber has different approaches to their caucuses. The House, with its much larger group of members, takes many hours to thoroughly chew through the bills. While the caucus setting is relatively informal, the Caucus Chair wields a gavel and must recognize members who hope to speak. The Speaker may exhort members to be team players; passionate words and sharp debates often break out, and it can feel sometimes like a group therapy session. The Senate's caucuses are generally less raucous and not as lengthy since the Senate has half the number of members as the House.

Members will plod through dozens of "good little bills" with committee chair descriptions that could put a baby to sleep, but the stuffy air sharpens instantly when one of the controversial bills is brought up. Members reengage and ask probing questions to flesh out all sides of whatever controversy they have heard about. Amendments, both sitting "on the bar" (drafted and formally submitted) or unformed beyond a whisper, are considered and discussed until a kind of collective consciousness forms.

The fate of a controversial bill is usually known by the end of the caucus discussion on it. Often, a formal vote count will be taken, and the Majority Leader or Minority Leader or Speaker will decide the likely next step.

Sometimes the caucus discussion is the death knell for a bill, and it goes no further. Sometimes amendments are proposed in an effort to address concerns and rescue or resurrect a bill. Sometimes the bill falls into an uneasy limbo, hanging by a thread while advocates and lobbyists outside the chamber doors work desperately to find a path forward.

What's said in caucus is supposed to stay in caucus. Even cell phone photos from caucus are prohibited. Members are not supposed to be called out or identified as opposing or supporting a bill. Nevertheless, as former Senator George W. Scott[1] once observed, "the only secrets in the legislature are unspoken ones"—because the outlines of a caucus discussion on a big bill usually leak out, perhaps with a wink, nod, or innuendo. The skilled lobbyists outside the doors of the chambers have their own sources, and they always seem to unearth the gist, if not the detail, of the discussion about a client's cause. Then, too, a legislator might violate the confidentiality of the caucus and share information with others. I knew a member who would sit silently during caucus discussion and rarely express an opinion—but then the details of those cloistered discussions would be reported faithfully to the Minority Leader of the opposition caucus. That member's espionage shut down full and honest caucus discussions for several years until he finally chose to caucus with the other party. I have also seen members, in both the

A cluster of Senate Democrats watching a tight vote count on a laptop in 2013, when we were in the minority. (Note that I am the only woman legislator in the cluster.)

House and Senate, so at odds with their caucuses that they remained at their desks on the floor rather than sit in the caucus room with their colleagues. It seemed a lonely road.

Outside of the party caucuses in each chamber, ad hoc caucuses of like-minded members form and disperse from time to time. Every few years, there's an effort to create a women's caucus in Washington's legislature. Many other state legislatures have created formal women's caucuses, but not Washington. But sharpened partisan differences over abortion and sex education issues have created a divide among Democratic and Republican women lawmakers in Washington, diluting their voices on issues ranging from childcare to sexual harassment.

Other informal caucuses, based on issues or geography, help inform members and move issues forward. One informal caucus that has coalesced successfully in recent years is the Members of Color Caucus. With the increasing diversity of members in the legislature, the need to understand and represent the interests of our African American, Latina (x/o), and Asian American and Pacific Islander communities has become more important than ever.

The most disruptive caucus I ever dealt with was the Roadkill Caucus, a group of middle-of-the-road Democrats who felt the Democratic caucus was marginalizing their positions. There were just enough centrist Democrats to put the brakes on many legislative initiatives supported by progressives. This group morphed into the Majority Coalition Caucus (MCC). MCC made it so difficult to make real progress, or even manage the Washington Senate caucus and floor action, that the Majority Leader abruptly resigned shortly after a particularly disruptive session in 2012.[2]

"I move that the rules be suspended, that the second reading be considered the third, and Senate Bill 5775 be placed on final passage."

That is the hallowed motion uttered before the final debate and vote on the floor for a bill. Most bills won't get that far. Those that do will most likely pass the chamber. It is an extremely rare thing for a bill to be brought up for a final vote and then fail to pass. If that occurs, it is viewed as a failure to manage the floor and caucus—an embarrassment that can damage a Leader's or Speaker's future.

KEY TAKEAWAYS

- Caucus discussions need to be kept confidential for honest debate to occur.
- Bills that get brought up in caucus will live or die there.
- Credibility is built or eroded during caucus debates and discussions.
- Informal caucuses have no institutional standing but can be very influential.

NOTES

1. George W. Scott, *A Majority of One: Legislative Life* (Seattle: Civitas Press, 2002), 154.
2. Jonathan Brunt, "Brown Won't Seek Another Senate Term," *Spokesman Review*, May 4, 2012.

CHAPTER 7

Across the Aisle

"It is not only important but mentally invigorating to discuss political matters with people whose opinions differ radically from one's own."
—Eleanor Roosevelt

When I first got to the legislature in 1995, most moderate Republican women were still pro-choice. There was no formal women's caucus, but we did gather occasionally, Democrats and Republicans alike, to share drinks and stories and strategies.

The women who had been in the legislature before or shortly after the 1992 Year of the Woman called themselves the MOB—which stood for Mean Old Bitches. They were tough, strong, amazing women. Ida Ballasiotes, Maryann Mitchell, and Shirley Winsley were some of the Republican members who were part of the pro-choice MOB, along with amazingly able Democratic lawmakers like Helen Sommers, Ruth Fisher, Mary Margaret Haugen, and Valoria Loveland. In the parlance of the day, they proudly considered themselves "tough old broads."

That was then, and I confess I'm rather nostalgic about those times and those women. The ground has shifted since, and it is dogma now for Republican women to be strictly anti-abortion and anti-choice.

The Washington state House has ninety-eight members, the Senate forty-nine, and each chamber has a distinct culture. Both chambers have a wide center aisle, with the bulk of each caucus sitting on one side or the other, depending on which side holds the majority of seats. In the wings off the side of each chamber is a room for caucusing—the party in the majority has the larger caucus room to accommodate its larger membership.

Working across the aisle, though less frequent than it once was, is a long-valued practice in the Senate. In the House, it is much rarer, and party-line votes on major bills are common.

While there is a world of difference between our U.S. Senate and House of Representatives in Washington, DC, and our state Senate and House in

Olympia, they enjoy many of the same conceits. George Washington is said to have told Thomas Jefferson, "We pour our legislation into the senatorial saucer to cool it," and a similar approach can be found in our state Senate. In contrast to the stodgy and dull upper chamber, meanwhile, both the U.S. House and state House are common havens for bold and brash ideologues.

With twice as many members, the House caucus leadership on both sides of the aisle has traditionally been paternalistic, sending a clear message to members to stick with the caucus position on bills—or else. Although an overt threat is never clearly articulated, the potential for serious political consequences makes it all the more trepidatious to consider crossing the aisle on a big bill where every vote is counted and closely watched. When a member from the House is appointed or elected to a seat in the Senate, he or she is often referred to as "House-broken." It is not meant as a compliment.

Three floor conversations taking place simultaneously, 2013. In the forefront, Senator Paul Shin, the only Korean American in the Washington state legislature at the time, is talking with Senator Steve Conway. In the middle, I am speaking with Republican Senator Bruce Dammeier, who is now the Pierce County Executive. We are discussing the Capital Budget. Behind us are Senator Curtis King, Republican from Yakima, and Democratic Senator Tracey Eide from Federal Way, likely talking about the Transportation Budget, as at that time Senator King was chair of the Transportation Budget and Senator Eide wanted an overpass for the connection of Interstate 5 and Highway 18, which eventually did get built.

Nevertheless, most bills in a legislative session are not strictly partisan. Dozens of "good little bills" that often amount to housekeeping or updating existing laws can provide opportunities to build bridges across the aisle. Bridges that build trust and respect are necessary for a successful legislative career. To pass major legislation you hope will stand the test of time, bipartisan support is usually needed.

For example, when I started on my quest to achieve paid family and medical leave, it was considered a fairly radical proposal. Eventually, I persuaded two Republicans to vote for the bill in the Senate on the first version that passed in 2007, only to see it amended into a dead-end "study bill" in the House. It took nearly another decade for the landmark legislation to pass into law. Senate Democrats were in the minority at the time, so they were dependent on Republican support and leadership to negotiate an agreed-to bill that won solid bipartisan backing. The Washington State Family and Medical Leave Act[1] has been successfully implemented and today offers a template on how to achieve significant change and provide true improvement for the people of the state. But it took intense negotiations and weeks of back-and-forth bargaining to get it done. A huge amount of groundwork by advocates and the threat to take the issue to the ballot as an initiative helped too.

Left, floor negotiations with Senator John Braun, 2015.
Right, floor discussion with Republican budget chair Andy Hill, 2013. Both photos show floor negotiations with Republican chairmen of the Senate Ways and Means committee when Democrats were in the minority. Senator Andy Hill, a very smart and popular Senator, passed away in 2016 from lung cancer, just a few years after he was elected into the Senate. Senator Braun is still on Ways and Means, and is now the Republican Minority Leader.

Left, I am speaking with Republican Senator Randi Becker, who took over as chair of the Senate Health Care Committee when Republicans regained control of the Senate and I became the ranking member of the Health Care Committee.
Right, I discuss strategy with Democratic Senator Rebecca Saldaña. Senator Saldaña assumed office in late 2016 to replace Pramila Jayapal, who had been elected to the U.S. House of Representatives.

When we were working on health care reform, the issue became very partisan. Once the Affordable Care Act (colloquially known as Obamacare) was passed in 2009, the effort to implement it fully in Washington state eventually led to the creation of the Washington State Health Exchange. It was a difficult fight. In 2011, we finally passed SB 5445, establishing the exchange, but only by a slim twenty-seven to twenty-two vote in the Senate, where twenty-five votes are necessary for passage. It wouldn't have made it without the help of Senator Cheryl Pflug, a registered nurse and a Republican member on the Senate Health Care Committee. Pflug later voted for marriage equality as well, and faced with an increasingly hostile Republican caucus, she left the Senate not long afterward.

Sadly, extreme partisanship is a growing divide that threatens constructive legislative solutions. It is less glaring in state legislatures than in Congress, but unfortunately the divide on ideological issues, such as reproductive rights and climate change, seems to be growing wider. I've heard a Republican state legislator from West Virginia say they get their party-line talking points every morning from Washington, DC.

Despite the sense of frustration and resignation that settles on a caucus when struggling with partisan disputes, it pays to try to forge agreement. Every member brings his or her own special expertise, life experiences, and interests that can inspire new energies for bipartisan effort. But it takes reaching out, building trust, and good-faith efforts, sometimes over many years. It doesn't always work. But sometimes it does.

In 2016, Senate Democrats were again in the minority, and I was assigned to the Senate Labor and Commerce Committee as its ranking member. (That means you are the lead committee member from the minority party, the much less powerful counterpart to the committee chair from the majority party who controls the committee and its agenda.)

In this case, the chair was a bright and profoundly conservative Republican and so anti-labor that he introduced a so-called "right-to-work" bill to severely undercut union rights in workplaces across the state.[2] His bill provoked one of the biggest protest rallies from union members in years, which I suspect was his goal—perhaps he wanted the attention more than the bill, which had precious little chance of passage.

Meanwhile, I introduced a bill to accommodate pregnant women in the workplace by according to them the right to sit while at work, to take needed restroom breaks, and to be assigned lighter-duty tasks as appropriate. As a father of several children, the chair had at least some knowledge of the temporary physical issues faced by some pregnant women, including his wife, and he recognized the merits of my bill.

Working together, we were able to negotiate a Pregnancy Accommodation Act. The sweetener came when I accepted the Republicans' opposition to having the act enforced by the state agency that monitors labor standards. We agreed instead that the state attorney general would be the enforcement agency. Well guess what? The AG is a very proactive and strong enforcement agency, and the first few years of the law's existence have seen dozens of cases resolved in favor of pregnant employees. Pregnancy accommodation is now an accepted workplace standard and employer obligation in our state. This "Healthy Starts Act" had its first trial victory in January of 2021, when FedEx contractor Sarai Alhasawi asked to be relieved of the requirement to lift 50-pound boxes because of her pregnancy. Her manager refused and fired her. Alhasawi's case was prosecuted by the AG in court, and the judge ordered her employer to not only pay all back wages and expenses but also $25,000 for emotional distress.

Another good example of bipartisan negotiations came during our efforts, over several years, on ways to curb cost increases for prescription drugs. In 2014, we passed the All Payer Claims Database as a first step to get real cost data on what we are paying for in health care.[3] In 2019, we passed the Prescription Transparency Act, which requires disclosure of prescription drug costs at every step of the way to the patient. But still, the price of insulin—a drug hundreds of thousands of diabetics have relied on daily for their survival for decades—continues to increase.

Working with the formidable House chair of health care, Representative Eileen Cody, we devised a strategy to get two key bills passed into law. Representative Cody is a master of working with her Republican health care committee members and winning their support. On this issue, she had developed legislation to curb the unwarranted price increases for insulin—but instead of sponsoring the bill herself, she invited a young Republican lawmaker with a son who had recently been diagnosed with Type 1 diabetes to sponsor it. The issue resonated with Representative Jacquelin Maycumber, and she championed the legislation passionately in the House.

Meanwhile, I had two related bills moving through the Senate floor. One, to cap insulin out-of-pocket costs, passed on a vote of thirty-four to fourteen with only Republicans voting in opposition. But when Representative Maycumber's insulin bill came over to the Senate, it passed unanimously. The difference? Legislators early in their careers need to build a record of effectiveness, and Republicans were willing to put aside their ideological reservations to give their young colleague a clear-cut accomplishment she could tout when running for reelection.[4]

Here's another example. For decades, the legislature had been in an argument with itself—based not on partisan lines but on a constituent and personal level—about the future of the large institutional residential care system for a small part of the state's intellectually and developmentally disabled (I/DD) community. While about 800 I/DD clients were receiving long-term residential care at our four large Residential Habilitation Center campuses, some 12,000 eligible I/DD clients were receiving no state-funded services. Complicating the dispute was a change in federal policy to support community-based care rather than institution-based care. Since the care is paid through a fifty-fifty share of state and federal funding, the loss of federal dollars would have decimated our residential centers. It was both a budget threat and a threat to the families and stakeholders who wanted to keep their loved ones in the familiar lodgings where they had lived for decades. Into this highly emotional and costly dispute, I worked with my Republican colleague, Senator John Braun, to engage in an eighteen-month dialogue with all parties to reach an agreement.

John and I worked together in good faith to pass a legislative seal of approval bill on the recommended solutions and to begin a funding shift in our operating budget to provide enhanced community care as well as more appropriate care for elderly clients who needed skilled nursing care. This was a long slog of a process, and ultimately we turned to the William D. Ruckelshaus Center—a mediation service through the University of Washington and Washington State University named after Watergate hero and Washington state resident Bill Ruckelshaus—to help resolve decades of acrimony and disputes. In the end, the votes in both chambers were nearly unanimous.[5]

In 2021, I was eager to work with the United Farmworkers Union to sponsor a new overtime pay law for farmworkers. When the original Fair Labor Standards Act (FLSA), establishing overtime, was proposed by President Roosevelt in the 1930s, Southern Senators refused to vote for it unless farmworkers and domestic workers were exempted, and they were. Farmworkers in the South then were mostly African American and now farmworkers are also Latina (o/x). When our state Supreme Court ruled in 2020 that dairy farms had to pay overtime to dairy employees, it opened the door to introduce a bill to extend overtime to all farmworkers in Washington state.

The hearings on SB 5172 had to be held virtually because of the pandemic, and hundreds of farmworkers, farmers, and lobbyists testified. The negotiations were long, difficult, and delicate. But by the end of the session, we were able to pass the bill with a three-year phase-in period to provide overtime pay for farmworkers. "SB 5172 will erase a racist legacy and correct an injustice that has existed for too long," said Larry Brown, president of the Washington State Labor Council. President Biden sent a statement of congratulations to the Legislature and Governor, saying this bill would help more than 100,000 farmworkers secure the overtime pay they deserved.

In keeping with my favorite baseball analogy, "you gotta have heart," hope springs eternal in every training camp and new legislative session. It's not easy to hit a grand slam in a legislative chamber, but there have been times when it's seemed possible. Usually you can at least get to second base. And at the beginning of every session, it's not uncommon for lawmakers to think, "This bill will be the one. This session will be the one."

Hope is a wonderful thing.

KEY TAKEAWAYS

- Being in the minority is difficult, but deals can still get done.
- Being in the majority is better, but getting support from at least a couple of members of the minority will make your bill stronger.
- Persist—but avoid being repetitive.
- When you have the majority, use it to make real change that will last, even if the minority wins the next election.

NOTES

1. On June 30, 2017, Senate Bill 5975 passed the Senate on a bipartisan vote of 37–12 and was passed by the House on a vote of 65–29 during the longest legislative session in state history.

2. SB 5671, "An act relating to the payment of union dues by partial public employees."

3. The original All-Payer Claims Database law was passed in 2014 and was amended in 2015 and 2019. In 2019, the Prescription Drug Transparency Act (HB1224, SB5292) became law. In 2020, SB 6087 became law, capping out-of-pocket insulin costs; HB 2662 also became law and created the Total Cost of Insulin Work Group to explore the potential of a state agency acting as a drug wholesaler or pharmacy benefit manger or purchaser of insulin. In 2021, SB 5203, to produce, distribute, and purchase insulin and generic drugs was passed into law. Prescription drugs are a multi-year project: see Chapter 18 on lobbyists, "Gucci Loafers."

4. In 2023, the Legislature passed SB 5729, making the cap permanent, with just one 'no' vote.

5. SB 6032, passed into law in 2018, established the Ruckleshaus Center to mediate stakeholders to rethink and transition Intellectual and Developmental Disability Policy to Empower Clients, Develop Providers, and Improve Services. SB 6419, passed in 2020, undertakes the implementation process for the I/DD transformation.

CHAPTER 8

Beyond the Chambers

"If there is no struggle, there is no progress."
—Frederick Douglass

New legislators arrive in their legislative chambers with the wind at their backs from successful campaigns. At a time when every impulse is telling you to focus on what's ahead of you, I warn you not to forget what's behind you—one of your key jobs as a new legislator is to keep your campaign allies and supporters connected with you.

The rush of legislative duties can distract, but always remember it wasn't just your own effort that got you elected to the legislature. You had lots of help! In other words: "Don't forget to dance with the one that brung ya."[1]

Washington state has strict restrictions against mixing legislative work with campaign activities. Staff, office, and any other state-issued resources, from laptops to cell phones, are paid for by taxpayers and cannot be used in any way to campaign for or influence an election. If you want to discuss non-legislative activities and concerns, you must go off campus and use a personal phone during personal time—during a lunch hour or a break in the workday or evening.

Some advocacy groups hold weekly meetings to provide updates and share strategies. Some lobbyists have access to generous expense accounts to wine and dine you (although Washington state members must abide by the legislative ethics committee's cap of a dozen dinners per year). Even though members are not allowed to accept contributions to their campaigns during a legislative session, sometimes promises of future support are suggested.

Or maybe you just meet up for an early-morning coffee or a late-night drink. Receptions, sometimes two or three a night, provide additional merry-go-rounds within the social-political circus. Some members keep a careful distance, some choose to engage only with friends, and others try to build a few bridges.

Beyond lobbyists, constituents, and advocates, members also need to connect with key people in the executive branch, from the governor on down. Dropping a bill before talking to agency staff, directors, or someone on the governor's staff can be risky. If your proposed law is a really big new idea, those agencies that would be affected might see it as a threat. Agencies are careful to guard their missions and their budgets—and they resist going outside what their governor wants to do. Getting beyond those limits can be a stretch that takes time. Just think of that stretch as an analogy for groundwork for your next challenge.

When we were pushing forward on health reform and developing our state's health exchange to implement Obamacare, we worked with a big table of health care advocates. We sat down with representatives from the governor's office, the state insurance commissioner's office, health insurance plans, hospitals, doctors, nurses, unions, and grass roots groups—it was a large and diverse stakeholder table. Together they called themselves "Healthy Washington," and they worked hard to help pass the Affordable Care Act in Congress and then to fully implement it through legislation at the state level.

As chair of the Senate Health Care Committee at the time, I worked day and night along with the advocates, and we were successful in passing legislation to create our Washington Health Exchange and to eventually reduce our state's uninsured population from 16 percent to 5 percent.

The state health exchange wasn't perfect, but it helped thousands of people purchase affordable health coverage or sign up for expanded Medicaid coverage, and it saved people's lives. In fact, our state exchange enabled people to access health care coverage under Obamacare faster and easier than in any other state and was soon seen as a model for the nation.

Doing big stuff can require collaboration with some strange bedfellows, and sometimes they're not folks you are all that comfortable working with. When we were negotiating our state's Paid Family and Medical Leave Act, legislators from both parties and both chambers personally participated in just about every meeting.

Business interests and unions and women's advocates faced each other across the table and stuck to good-faith negotiations to get to "yes." The two to four lawmakers in attendance mostly observed but sometimes asked questions or suggested everyone take a break to talk things over when necessary. It took an immense amount of time and commitment.

We happened to be at a budget impasse. We had a divided Legislature and Republicans controlled the Senate at that time, so we had the luxury of additional time to hash it all out during the extra legislative sessions it took to settle the budget. It also helped that the labor and women's advocates had rock-solid polling in hand showing that if they took the issue to the ballot with an initiative, voters would pass it. Just two years earlier, voters had passed our state's universal sick leave and minimum wage increase through a decisive ballot initiative. The political threat was real and served to keep less-enthused participants at the table.

Working with advocates takes time. Building off the successful family and medical leave law, seniors advocates and unions coalesced around a similar proposal to create the Long Term Care Trust Act. Using a grassroots approach, the campaign employed meetings between seniors and their legislative representatives back home in their districts between sessions.

Our state's Senior Lobby, AARP, and the Alliance for Retired Americans, along with unions representing home care workers and long-term care providers, lined up in support of a proposed payroll tax paid by employees which would capitalize a trust fund to pay for long-term care. It was helpful that businesses didn't oppose the idea. Actuarial studies, hearings, polling, and research were all used to put the necessary pieces in place to move the proposed legislation forward over a period of three years. Legislators felt little threat of immediate backlash and realized that, among their constituents, senior-age voters are the most dependable.

This all goes to show that no one lawmaker can change the world without help from others—indeed, many others. Lawmaking can be frustrating, but when broad collaboration and smart strategy come together, real change can happen.

NOTES

1. Texas coach Darrell Royal coined the phrase that writer Molly Ivins used in her 1998 book title, *You Got to Dance with Them What Brung Ya*, about President Clinton.

CHAPTER 9

In the Margins

"As a black person, I am no stranger to prejudice. But the truth is, in the political world, I have been far oftener discriminated against because I am a woman than because I am black."
—U.S. Representative Shirley Chisholm, May 21, 1969

A fine line for newly elected legislators who are women or people of color, or both, is to fully voice their concerns and perspectives while avoiding being marginalized. The danger is that those who repeat the same refrain too many times can become pigeonholed. But how many times is too many? The trick is to establish a voice for a particular community or group, which has great value, without becoming narrowly defined by that group, which will limit your effectiveness on other issues.

Tokenism is another dangerous space. Individuals who allow themselves to be used as tokens can enable an institution to pretend it values diversity without actually doing anything. It takes hard, concerted effort for an institution to incorporate truly diverse perspectives, all the more so in tradition-bound institutions such as legislatures. As good progressives, we all try to invite and value diversity and to avoid tokenism and marginalization. And we need to be called out when we misstep.

New members who join a legislature after working for or participating with advocates need to undergo the mental shift from working as an outsider to an insider. I learned that as I went from working for the state AFL-CIO to representing a suburban district of 120,000 people where about 48 percent of the voters did not vote for me in my first election.

U.S. Representative Pramila Jayapal also experienced that transition from activism in her first state Senate session. "Our movement had become so accustomed to our own form of internalized oppression," she later observed. "We were not part of the power structure, and so this was a continuation of that 'us-versus-them' mentality. Having our own people in positions of power required both a mental shift and a restructuring of the way we did things."

Pramila had led the One America organization for years before winning election to the state Senate, and she continues to fight for the goals of that movement in her current congressional seat.[1]

Another woman of color, Senator Rosa Franklin, was for many years the only Black woman in the Washington Senate and was constantly called on to represent her race and her position at countless events.[2] It must have been so tiring for her, but she never complained! I worked closely with Rosa, and I knew she fully understood she was an important symbol of hope and aspiration for others, but she never allowed herself to be used as a token. Though some members may have viewed her simplistically as "the only one," Rosa knew exactly who she was—a role model for Black Americans and a champion for her constituents regardless of color or creed—and her self-awareness and sense of humor gave her an unfailingly bold and authentic voice.

Those qualities were never on better display than in the aftermath of a heated stakeholder meeting in 2004 that erupted in an ugly racial epithet. In one of a seemingly endless series of meetings with health care negotiators, the Senate Health Care Committee chair had lost his temper and called a House member "a n----- in the woodshed." Though the House member happened to be white, the racist nature of the slur was unmistakable. Senator Franklin was not a witness to the outburst, but as the sole Black member of the Senate, she dutifully accepted the burden of defusing a painfully racist incident. In a high-stakes moment on the Senate floor, Rosa acknowledged and accepted the senator's tearful apology with characteristic grace. But she also said this:

> I am a descendant of slaves, with French and Native-American heritage. I am from a family who have stood up for the rights of the least of us, regardless of who you are, the color of your skin, we have stood up. I am a family from a heritage that have felt the lashes of horse whips, who toiled in the cotton fields and rice paddies of South Carolina, yet we have become nurses, teachers, pharmacists, doctors, and we have stood up for everyone. I accept Senator Deccio's apology and will work for healing. This is what this country needs.... Race does matter in America. We don't want to talk about it, but it does matter.

Rosa was a role model for me. She stood her ground. As a white woman who grew up in a tiny Iowa farming town—where there was not one person of color, where the only breaks in homogeneity were between Catholics, Lutherans, and Methodists, and between those with German accents and those with Swedish ones—my parochial world was blown apart during college. This was during the tumultuous decade of the 1960s at University of California, Berkeley, and what I heard and saw and experienced gifted me with a much more inclusive perspective. I learned so much. And, yet, I know I still have so much more to learn as our society looks more honestly and openly at the realities of race and diversity.

Senator Rosa Franklin and I catch up on the floor, 2007. Rosa served as our caucus conscience and as Senate President Pro Tempore before she retired in 2011.

In 1996, when I first ran for office, my legislative district was mostly suburban white and middle class, though it was just beginning to change. One of its six suburban cities was a small enclave of white, upper middle-class Republicans where voter turnout was so high you couldn't win the district if you didn't make a significant dent in those neighborhoods. But as the cost of living in Seattle grew, the more affordable suburbs drew Black and Asian families.

The Sea-Tac International Airport community became a magnet for newly arriving immigrants from Africa and Asia, and other areas acquired large Latina (x/o) communities, to the point that my district is now one of the most diverse in the state while also possessing the lowest income and highest poverty rates in the county. It is a joy and privilege to experience and learn from communities with such a rich cultural and racial heritage; it is also my responsibility to make sure the voices and concerns of those varied communities are heard and addressed by our legislature. It is also a constant struggle to win equitable funding with the higher-income communities surrounding us.

These days, members of the LGBTQ community, the Latinx community, the AAPI community, the African American community, and the women's rights and trans communities all have a larger and stronger presence in our legislative chambers and caucuses and lead with strong voices for the betterment of our state and our constituents.

Still, it is up to all of us to encourage and amplify these voices—not just in the chambers but at leadership tables and at the committee chair level of our legislatures. The progress we have realized up to now is but the beginning of a long march. We must not allow voices to be marginalized or tokenized by a reversion to "business as usual" or a failure to continue pressing for further enlightenment. And enlightenment is badly needed.

"Being successful in a system that was not built for people like us entailed navigating unwritten rules while putting up with behavior one might find in a high school cafeteria," observed first-time Senator Joe Nguyen. "It's like having to hear other senators ridicule your last name on the Senate floor during your first speech or feeling like you aren't doing enough while working twice as hard as most other members."

Active recruitment for candidates with a lens toward racial and gender diversity should be required of caucus campaign committees.

Institutional traditions and systemic racism will change only through intentional acts of outreach to communities of color, recruitment of people with diverse lived experience, and with a broader perspective that includes an equity lens.

KEY TAKEAWAYS

People of color, especially women, have the additional burden to speak for and represent those communities as well as their district.

Recruitment and advancement are key actions needed to correct the imbalance of race and gender in legislatures.

Racism, overt and subtle, must be addressed forthrightly and openly.

We can do this. Even more importantly, we must do this.

NOTES

1. Pramila Jayapal, *Use the Power You Have: A Brown Woman's Guide to Politics and Political Change* (New York: The New Press, 2020), 81.

2. Tamiko Nimura, *Rosa Franklin: A Life in Heath Care, Public Service, and Social Justice* (Olympia: Washington State Oral History Program, 2019), 75.

CHAPTER 10

Passing the Torch

"In 1972, the year I was elected, there had only been eight women in the House and no women in the Senate! It was largely the good old boys' club."
—Representative Helen Sommers

Legislative leadership in America has been a white male-dominated enclave for more than two centuries. In most legislative buildings, old photographs of previous members, caucuses, and leadership hang all over the walls—and for generations they were photographs of white men—men with beards, men with mustaches, all men.

When Black men won the right to vote after the Civil War, they turned out in huge numbers. "Slavery is not abolished, until the Black man has the ballot," Frederick Douglass said in 1865, a month after the Union victory at Appomattox. Twenty-two Black men were elected to Congress, and dozens more were elected across the South in state and municipal elections during Reconstruction. By 1870, Congress passed the Fifteenth Amendment to the U.S. Constitution, which said that voting rights could not be "denied or abridged by the United States or by any state on account of race, color or previous condition of servitude."

Nevertheless, the Jim Crow era was born, and literacy tests, poll taxes, and other voting restrictions were implemented across the South to limit the rights of Black Americans to vote. It wasn't until 1965, when Lyndon B. Johnson pushed the Voting Rights Act through Congress, that those restrictions were rolled back.

Even after women won the right to vote just over a century ago, few women were elected to the country's state legislatures or to Congress. In some states, such as Washington, women won and lost and then won again the right to vote locally by 1910. But it took another decade for the required thirty-eight states to ratify the proposed constitutional amendment granting women the right to vote.

It all seems like ancient history, but white male privilege still lingers in legislatures. It's been slow progress for women and people of color over the last century. In 2020, less than 30 percent of the country's 7,383 state legislators were women. Only 25 percent of those 2,145 women were women of color. Nearly 68 percent of all women legislators were Democrats. Nevada became the first and only state legislature with a majority of women lawmakers, with 52.4 percent in 2020. Voting is the first right of any democracy, but it isn't an immediate remedy for generations of discrimination.

The Nineteenth Amendment to the U.S. Constitution made it legal for most American white and Black women to vote in 1920, but legal barriers persisted. Until 1922, an American woman could not vote if she was married to an immigrant. Even after 1922, American women remained disenfranchised if married to an Asian immigrant. Native Americans—women and men alike—had no voting rights until 1924.

Senator John McCoy, one of the few Native Americans in the Washington state legislature, stops by for a chat on the floor, 2018.

Senator Manka Dhingra and I conducting floor negotiations in 2018. The Democrats gained a one-vote majority that year as a result of her election to office.

Western states were ahead of the rest of the country in the fight for women's suffrage. In 1894, the first three women elected to a state legislature in the nation were all elected to the Colorado House of Representatives. Two years later, in Utah, Martha Hughes Cannon became the first woman elected as a state senator anywhere in the country. In 1912, following the 1910 state law giving women the right to vote, the first two women were elected to the Washington State House of Representatives—Frances C. Axtell from Bellingham and Nena J. Croake from Tacoma.

It wasn't until 1943 that then-Congressman Warren G. Magnuson championed a law that allowed Chinese immigrants to become naturalized citizens with the right to vote. It took nearly another decade, however, for Congress to pass the McCarran-Walter Act in 1952, which extended the same rights to Japanese and Korean immigrants. Sadly, our country has a long history of restricting certain people's right to vote.

And here we are again: after a flurry of false claims of voter fraud in the 2020 defeat of Donald Trump, Republicans in state after state introduced dozens of bills to restrict voting. By May of 2021, fourteen states had enacted twenty-two separate bills into law to restrict voting. This new era of voter suppression seems like déjà vu all over again, except that progressive states

The 1925 roster of Washington state senators included Reba J. Hurn, the first woman elected to the state Senate. She joined the Senate in 1923 and served two terms.

are fighting back. According to the Brennan Center's update, nearly thirty bills to *expand v*oting rights have been passed into law in another fourteen states in 2021.[1]

A century ago, as women began to increase their participation in civic life—through the League of Women Voters, through the rise of expanding unions' workplace democracy, and through more access to higher education—they also began to run and win office. Many started first on school boards and city councils, then progressed to the state legislature. Leadership, including control of budgets, remained out of reach, however.

In Washington in 1954, Julia Butler Hansen of Cathlamet was nearly elected the first female Speaker of the Washington State House, falling just a few votes short. She surely would have been disappointed and shocked to learn that more than fifty years would pass before Representative Laurie Jinkins would become the first female Speaker of the House in Washington state in 2020.

Why did it take so long? We neglected to pass the torch. Just 5 percent of state lawmakers were women in 1971, but our ranks grew steadily until about 1995, when growth stalled. We maintained our participation at between 20 and 25 percent but didn't significantly increase our numbers. It's my opinion that we failed to build the kind of pipeline that's been in place for so many successful male legislators. Creating an infrastructure of support, mentoring, networking, and fundraising are all needed to build and maintain an open pipeline for women—especially women of color and young women—to enter the fantastic career of politics and lawmaking. But women of color bear an additional burden: the double blind of racism and sexism. In 1991, Kimberlé Williams Crenshaw was one of the first to explore this hybrid phenomenon in which the two forms of bigotry—sexism and racism—intersected and came to be called, logically, "intersectionality."

Gender presents a factor all its own. When women are asked to run for political office, their first reaction is often something on the order of, "I'm not a politician! I don't have the experience or training! I couldn't possibly ask anyone for money to fund my campaign!" Or variations on those themes. Consultants say it takes at least seven asks to get a woman to decide she can run for office. Most men, they say, don't wait for anyone to ask; they jump in with both feet running, confident they will succeed and proceed to higher office in due time.

At one time, from 1993 to 2004, Washington state's legislature led the country in electing women, boasting the highest percentage of women legislators in the nation. Coming on the heels of the 1992's Year of the Woman election, the ranks of women lawmakers swelled to 41 percent of the legislature in Washington state. But by 2010, after many retirements and some election losses, the percentage of women members fell to about a third. During that same period, many of the more moderate Republican women were replaced with staunchly conservative and antiabortion Republican women.

Numbers alone don't tell the whole story. The Washington State Legislature became a lonely place for progressive women during that time. In any caucus, it takes a solid percentage of members who are aligned with progressive values in order to wield real leverage on caucus positions. When the number of women in our Senate Democratic Caucus plunged from eighteen to six, progressive issues stalled. Progress is not always linear.

The last decade has seen one major female figure rise to the stature of a historic legislative leader in the U.S. Congress—Nancy Pelosi, who was the first woman to be elected Speaker of the House and later the first woman to be reelected when the Democrats regained the House majority in 2018. As Lyndon B. Johnson was once called the "Master of the Senate," Nancy Pelosi has become the "Master of the House." ("Mistress" just doesn't work!) More recently, a few women governors have made their mark, but legislative leadership remains rare, with only eight women in our fifty state legislatures serving as Speaker.

Gender equity isn't an end in itself, of course. But many studies have shown that having women in leadership, whether in the private sector or the public sector, creates more successful results.[2]

For progressives in state legislatures, it can mean winning new rights and protecting hard-fought gains. It means better funding for public schools, health care, and social services. It means stronger protections against pay discrimination, domestic abuse, and hate crimes. All of these goals are within reach through state legislative action with strong progressive women lawmakers taking the lead and serving in leadership positions.

To that end, any woman aspiring to public office should be encouraged by the example of U.S. House Speaker Nancy Pelosi. Pelosi didn't run for federal office until she was forty-seven and the mother of five children, though she was a very active Democrat in California politics. She won election to Congress from her San Francisco district in 1987, well before the Year of the Woman in 1992 and the Republican rout led by Newt Gingrich's "Contract with America" in 1994.

As the U.S. Representative from San Francisco during the AIDS epidemic, Pelosi fought for legislation to address AIDS and combat homophobia. A staunch Roman Catholic, she defended reproductive choice from constant attack. She joined the caucus leadership team after successfully running for whip, the person who tracks where everyone stands on controversial bills and "whips" the votes. Having learned the vital lesson of how to count votes in that role, she went on to run for and win the job of Speaker of the House in 2007.

Pelosi used her position to champion the Lilly Ledbetter Fair Pay Act on sex discrimination, and she famously drew a line in the sand when Rahm Emanuel, President Obama's chief of staff, wanted to cave on comprehensive health reform and limit coverage to children only. Pelosi insisted that the comprehensive Affordable Care Act would pass Congress intact, and she made sure it did.

"I've always been confident," she said as she saved Obamacare from the incrementalists who wanted to settle for what she termed "kiddie care."

As Speaker, Pelosi was targeted in a nasty GOP branding campaign in 2010, labeled as a latte-loving, San Francisco liberal and slammed with unflattering photos and personal attacks in a heavily-funded, Tea Party-fueled fury. When Democrats lost the majority in that election, Pelosi had to hand the gavel back to the Republicans in 2011. It wasn't until 2019 that she once again counted her votes to defeat challengers in her own caucus and regain the Speaker's gavel. Her vaunted ability to be a tough negotiator and a courageous leader who never flinches defies comparison—she persists and she prevails.

"I've always been confident" might prove to be her most fitting epitaph. Perhaps that's an attitude we should all consider adopting.

KEY TAKEAWAYS

- Voting rights, suffrage for all, opens the door.
- White males enjoy the privilege and benefit of decades of decision-making in legislatures.
- Pipelines need to be built and maintained to help women and people of color to run and win so they can pass landmark laws.
- Progress is a continuum that must be expanded and defended from erosion or repeal as political winds change.

NOTES

1. Brennan Center. "Voting Laws Roundup: May 2021." Accessed March 21, 2021. https://www.brennancenter.org/our-work/research-reports/voting-laws-roundup-may-2021.

2. Bob Sherwin, "Why Women Are More Effective Leaders Than Men," *Business Insider*, January 24, 2014.

CHAPTER 11

#MeToo

"I cautiously went up to speak to the very powerful Speaker of the Missouri House of Representatives. And I explained to him the bill, and [asked] did he have any advice. And he looked at me, and he paused, and he said, 'Well did you bring your knee pads?'"
—U.S. Senator Claire McCaskill

It was just over a decade ago that an angry Democratic male senator threw a temper tantrum and called me a "cunt" and a "bitch" on the Senate floor when he couldn't get what he wanted.

It was only five years ago that a male state senator in Washington had to resign his seat in response to documented rumors of inappropriate behavior.[1]

In 2018, allegations of sexual harassment surfaced in state legislatures in Minnesota, Kentucky, Illinois, Rhode Island, and Oregon. Some 200 women in Sacramento signed a letter protesting a pervasive environment of sexual wrongdoing in the California statehouse.

Silence is the enemy of justice. Jeffrey Epstein, Bill Cosby, Harvey Weinstein, Bill O'Reilly, and R. Kelly were high-profile celebrities who were able to use sexual harassment and assault for years without repercussion.[2] No one believed the women who spoke out until the #MeToo movement broke the silence.

I came of age during the 1960s women's movement, when Gloria Steinem broke the inside story of the Hugh Hefner culture by working as a Playboy Bunny and telling her tale. It was the culture Donald Trump relished as he bragged in 2016 about being able to "grab them by the pussy." Sadly, sometimes it seems nothing ever changes.

The U.S. Supreme Court currently has two sitting justices—Clarence Thomas and Brett Kavanaugh—with highly credible accusations of sexual harassment and sexual assault leveled against them. Anita Hill in 1990 and Christine Blasey Ford in 2018 came forward and testified before Congress, but their accounts were dismissed by a majority of U.S. senators who voted to confirm lifetime appointments to the highest court in the land to men accused of sex crimes. Washington's U.S. Senator Patty Murray first ran for that office against an incumbent, Senator Brock Adams, who was facing accusations of date rape of a legislative staffer.

Sexism, misogyny, and patriarchy all aim to shame and intimidate women and girls. It is a means to an end of control and power over women, in domestic arrangements, in workplaces, and in legislatures. Sexism and racism are twin evils, and both must be outed whether by a #MeToo movement, the woman-led Black Lives Matter movement, or some new combination. But after the protests and marches, the real work is to change the law. And there is much work to be done.

As Ibram X. Kendi advises, "Changing minds is not a movement.... Changing minds is not activism. An activist produces power and policy change, not mental change. If a person has no record of power or policy change, then that person is not an activist."[3]

Policy changes are now occurring in some cities and state legislatures. Low-wage workers, especially immigrants and women of color working in hospitality and agriculture, are particularly vulnerable to workplace sexual harassment, assault, and rape.

Chicago and Seattle became the first cities to require hotels to provide panic buttons for housekeepers working alone with no surveillance or security when the Washington legislature passed my bill to expand the coverage for hotel housekeeper panic buttons statewide and also to include janitors and security guards. But we didn't have the votes to extend the protections to farmworkers. There's much work still to be done.

The police and justice system's failure to process thousands of rape kits is not only a failure of justice but an indication of disregard for the victim and a minimizing of the crime. In some states, including Washington, additional funding to process the backlog of untested rape kits is uncovering serial rapists who are being caught and charged with their multiple crimes. Nevertheless, the threat of sexual harassment, sexual assault, and rape still haunts all women of all races.

Non-disclosure agreements (NDAs) and mandatory arbitration clauses in workplace contracts create legal gag rules that prevent victims of sex or race discrimination from taking their cases to court. Pervasive use of NDAs creates a culture of silence that allows discrimination to thrive.[4]

"In my case, the sexual assault was terrible and traumatizing," said Liz Manne, a former movie executive for New Line Cinema. "But the worst part—the very worst part of it, the enduring part of it—is the gag order. This is 20 years of legally imposed silence."[5]

But the federal Arbitration Act preempts state legislatures from directly addressing this injustice. I was able to thread a legal needle by passing a bill into law that limits Washington state NDAs because states still have jurisdiction over contracts.[6]

Twenty-five years ago, Congress placed a cap on damages for individual discrimination cases. That cap has never been adjusted, much less lifted, and the limit makes discrimination a minor cost of doing business for a large corporation. Again, there is still so much work to be done!

KEY TAKEAWAYS

As told by Jennie Willoughby, ex-wife of former White House staffer Rob Porter, in response to President Trump calling her a liar:
"There are three things I know to be true:

- Where there is anger, there is underlying pain.
- Where there is denial, there is underlying fear.
- Where there is abuse, there is cover-up."

The twelve women holding seats in Senate Caucus 16, 2019. Note that one-third of the women are also people of color.

Portraits of the eight women holding office in the Washington State House of Representatives, 1971. Pictured in the top row (left to right) are Gladys Kirk, Peggy Joan Maxie, Lois North, and Marjorie W. Lynch; in the bottom row are (left to right) Lorraine Wojahn, Doris J. Johnson, Geraldine McCormick, and Margaret Hurley.

A gathering of the women serving as state Representatives in the House (less one), 1971. Representative Peggy Maxie was the only African American in the House. No woman held office in the state Senate in 1971, and Senator George Fleming was the only African American in the Senate.

NOTES

1. Associated Press, "Washington state Senator Kevin Ranker resigns amid misconduct accusations," *Seattle Times*, January 12, 2019. https://www.seattletimes.com/seattle-news/politics/washington-state-sen-kevin-ranker-resigns-as-misconduct-investigation-continues.

2. Jodi Kantor and Megan Twohey, *She Said: Breaking the Sexual Harassment Story That Helped Ignite a Movement* (London: Penguin Press, 2019), 182.

3. Ibram X. Kendi, *How to Be an Anti-Racist* (New York: One World, 2019), 209.

4. "Non-disclosure agreements with confidentiality clauses are supported by both defendants and some powerful legal representative of victims. The resulting secrecy allows predators to repeat their behaviors." Kantor and Twohey, *She Said*, 78.

5. "Silence is the Enemy of Justice," editorial, The Ms. Team, *Ms. Magazine*, January 2018: "Real change requires a series of new laws—starting with prohibiting the use of nondisclosure agreements in legal settlements and ending mandatory confidential arbitration clauses in employment clauses." Linda Burstyn, "The Weinstein Effect" *Ms. Magazine*, January 2018.

6. "Preventing the sexual harassment and sexual assault of certain isolated workers" was the title of SB 5258, passed into law in 2019 to provide panic buttons and other workforce protections for hotel, motel, and retail workers or security guards who work in isolated settings. In 2018, the Washington State Legislature took a three-part approach to NDAs, passing SB 5996, SB 6313, and SB 6068, which all became law, limiting employers from requiring new employees to sign NDAs, voiding any employment contract that requires an employee to waive their right to file a complaint under antidiscrimination law or that requires mandatory arbitration—and voiding any NDA that limits legal discovery and witness testimony in civil lawsuits.

CHAPTER 12

Balancing Work and Family

"We need to do a better job of putting ourselves higher on our own to-do list."
—Michelle Obama

In 1993, when Lisa Brown was first elected to the Washington State Legislature, she was a single mom with a very young son. One night as the House floor debate ran late, after the baby's childcare facility had closed, Lisa brought her son to the floor and was scolded by the Speaker for doing so.[1] This triggered a statewide debate and brought to the forefront a dialogue about workplace and family issues.

That was almost thirty years ago. Today the legislature invites children and grandchildren to the floor for an annual Children's Day. When my youngest son came to the floor with me, he was able to help vote for a bill declaring the state insect following a floor debate over ladybugs and dragonflies (the Common Green Darner Dragonfly won the vote). Children's Day is a fun event, but it does nothing to address the work and family conflicts faced by lawmakers raising young children.

The worst conflict I ever had involved my son's surprise birthday party when he was just turning ten. We were in the minority at that time, so although I had to leave the floor to attend this special event, I would not ask to be formally excused—the vote count was close, and I didn't want to alert Republicans to an opportunity by having it announced that I was excused. The ploy didn't quite work. I got to my son's party on time, but the Republicans noticed I had left and brought up an important anti-labor bill I strongly opposed. It passed, and I felt an awful guilt.

In 2005, Lisa Brown became the first Democratic female to be elected Senate Majority Leader in Washington state. Republican Jeannette Hayner had become the first woman to lead the Republican caucus in what the *Seattle Times* called a "startling upset" in 1979,[2] and she was subsequently elected Majority Leader in 1981, when the Republicans gained the majority in the Washington State Senate.[3] But Hayner never made family-friendly policies

Senator Lisa Brown and I in discussion on the floor, 2008. Senator Brown became the first female Senate Majority Leader in 2005 and we worked closely together on both legislation and politics.

part of the agenda, much less a priority (however, she did choose the lovely décor and couches for the women's lounge). Lisa Brown, in contrast, was a champion for paid family leave and many other family-friendly bills that became law. She also took care to manage floor sessions so our older senators' health wasn't compromised, maintaining a curfew of 10:00 p.m. for a time. The House tradition, by contrast, has always been to work into the wee hours of the morning.

"As a younger single mom, I was shocked at how many people would ask me 'Who's going to take care of your children when you're gone?' It underscored for me the challenges moms have to enter these institutions," said Senator Liz Lovelett. "Society is not set up for women to be both a leader and a 'good mom' but that's exactly who needs to be at the table when we're talking about schools, social programs, health care, childcare and budget priorities."

The problems of balancing work and family life remains a serious challenge for legislators today—and not only for women lawmakers with young children. Many a marriage has hit the rocks after a couple of sessions in those marbled chambers. It's something of an occupational disease—the privilege of serving is always evident, but the cost isn't.

Long, intense meetings on urgent, vital issues can spark strong emotions—sometimes anger, sometimes passion. Late-night floor debates, running, on occasion, as late as 3:00 or 4:00 a.m. can rub nerves raw with exhaustion—and then anger erupts at home. Endless hours in budget hearings that go on near the annual legislative cut-off deadline for twelve to fourteen hours creates a camaraderie and partnership among members that can develop into close relationships. After-session drinks and dinners can lead one astray. Weeks away from home, where winter weather makes it dangerous to travel back and forth, creates its own set of potential domestic tensions.

These are all typical ingredients in legislative sessions that have contributed to countless separations and divorces. The additional pressures of special sessions for emergency conditions only increase the tension and temptations. After my divorce, I started seeing a longtime lobbyist. We shared many interests, and I enjoyed his company. But the day when he walked in to testify on a bill during a Health Care Committee hearing that I was chairing, my stomach clenched into a knot and I suddenly realized I couldn't survive that kind of conflict. So that was the end of that relationship.

My eighteen-year marriage had become shaky when I was elected to the legislature. With no extended family in the area to help with our three kids, I had to depend on my husband. He worked on documentary projects from home, so initially it seemed doable. But resentments built, and at the end of one long week he presented me with a "timecard" where he showed me he'd been keeping a daily count of how many hours a day I was gone. For weeks afterwards, I avoided attending after-session receptions or social events and hit the road for home as soon as I could get away. The stress took its toll on both of us, and within three years we were separated. Two years later we were divorced.

Some members endure by jealously guarding their time, leaving on the dot at 6:00 p.m. for a two-hour drive to get home every night so that their kids will have their parent hug them goodnight and be there in the morning. Some members move their families to the Capitol during session, but that can disrupt the school year and a spouse's occupation. Young families face the most stress and difficulty, one of the reasons so many lawmakers are older, usually retired with grown children. I was serving when my kids were old enough to be dangerous—preteens and teens. Although they were "good kids," I had wonderful neighbors keeping an eye out. Still, I was startled one night when I discovered the screen of my fifteen-year-old daughter's bedroom window was off. Oh dear, the times we had!

Gender can make a big difference. Many male lawmakers have wives at home to manage the childcare duties. Female members rarely have a spouse willing or able to do so. A strong family-and-friend support system can be a good substitute. Any young new member with young children should arrange a safe, secure, and dependable support system for her kids and herself before she is sworn into office.

Remember how lucky I said I was to be a member of the minority party when I first joined the legislature? Having time to learn and observe is one benefit, but being in the minority also just means a lot less work. I could drive back and forth to the Capitol every day of session. I wasn't responsible for chairing committee hearings or setting agendas and didn't even have to participate in some of the long fiscal hearings. Being a member of the minority can be frustrating, but for members with young children, it can also make life a little easier to manage.

It helped that the Republican caucus didn't seem terribly interested in passing laws, and it usually adjourned and left town on Thursday nights. When Democrats got back in the majority, they kept a busy session with floor action lasting late into many evenings, and never took Fridays off. There was too much to get done!

Honest, open conversations with loved ones, children, parents, spouses, and partners need to be had before the maelstrom of session starts. As daunting and overwhelming as it often seemed, my three kids all grew up to be smart, loving, empathetic, and progressive adults.

Although I worried incessantly and felt awful guilt, the kids were just fine, and I think they actually grew to become more self-sufficient and independent because I wasn't a constant presence. Looking back now, I don't know how we all managed. But we did, and I am so incredibly thankful for the privilege, the good luck, and the blessings we were able to experience and enjoy.

KEY TAKEAWAYS

- If you have children, organize a strong support system of friends, family, and supporters before you are even sworn into office.

- If you have a spouse or partner who is supportive of your goals, don't forget to respond generously with your support and respect for your partner's.

- Be alert to the situational nature of many emotional feelings if you are involved in lengthy and intense encounters. Guard your vulnerabilities.

- Gossip will travel, and what you do in a session or at a legislative conference will become known and may be used against you.

NOTES

1. Erik Smith, "Senate Majority Leader Brown misses Senate vote when son involved in accident—a Onetime Legislative Celebrity Himself." *WashingtonStateWire.com*, February 4, 2011. Accessed March 21, 2023.

2. See https://en.wikipedia.org/wiki/Jeannette_C._Hayner.

3. Ibid.

CHAPTER 13

Finding Your Niche

"The most pathetic person in the world is someone who has sight but no vision."
—Helen Keller

After your first few sessions, you will discover where your real passion leads. Some members come to the legislature with a clear plan of action and focused personal goals. But most members arrive in a whirlwind of election euphoria and an "I can do this!" attitude.

I like that attitude and urge all new members to remain enthusiastic. Even if you are in the minority in a legislature, you can tap many methods to make your mark. As former Senator George W. Scott observed, "Freshmen enjoy in enthusiasm what they lack in power."[1] It is hard to not be disappointed or even discouraged when your first priority bill or budget allocation fails to pass into law. But one of the best things about annual legislative sessions is that there's always another session coming up to try again. Maybe you try a different approach, different language, different strategies, but persistence pays off in most cases.

I think of each session the way the baseball fan thinks of the opening game for the season. As the song goes, "You gotta' have heart, lots and lots and lots of heart..." To take the baseball analogy one more step, consider the resilient mindset in Lawrence's Thayer's legendary poem, "Casey at the Bat": Though there is "no joy in Mudville" at game's end, you sense the locals cannot help but return for the next game with renewed hope.[2] In this sense, legislating resembles baseball far more than other popular sports because you are playing the long game.

In his book, *Majority of One*, Senator Scott suggested that a newly elected legislator's most important act is to make good decisions early on about what they want to specialize in and then win appointment to the right committees for that specialization. And once you get the committee assignments you want, dig in and create your niche.

Every legislative chamber has numerous committees, sometimes too many, and new members should study the purview of a committee for the issues they hope to work on. For example, if improving special education is your passion, find out if such issues are more likely to be addressed by the Education Committee or by the Human Services Committee. Though a committee's name might imply a particular focus, that focus will reflect the priorities of the committee's chair, and every chair is different. So, too, are parties—it's not uncommon for a committee's emphasis to change radically when a new party seizes majority control and reshapes the committee's goals to mirror those of the party. If climate change is your passion, would your energies find more support on the Transportation Committee, on the Natural Resources Committee, or on the Environment and Energy Committee? Might one be a better fit than the other? Make your case to your caucus leaders and let them help you find your groove.

In time, as you discover your own legislative specialty, it makes sense to develop a sub-specialty, perhaps one of particular importance to your district. In my legislative career, I focused on two main issues: health care and labor, including the nexus of workplace safety and health, and I made those my main policy committees. But my district and my constituents are heavily impacted by the operation of the state's international airport in our backyard. Airport issues overlap with all kinds of committee jurisdictions, from state and local government to environment to transportation. Though I do not hold a seat on any of those committees, I have worked hard to build credibility on airport issues and cultivated effective relationships with members of those committees. As a result, my airport bills have received hearings and positive action in all of them. "Committees are the heart of the legislature," Scott declared, and I have to agree—if you want to make substantial, sustainable change, your work in committee is where it begins.

By making shrewd decisions about which committees you seek to serve on, you open doors to committee and caucus staff who can provide invaluable knowledge and experience. But don't simply rely on them to do your work for you, as capable as they may be. Specialize in the couple of key areas that are primary to your goals—dig deep, develop real knowledge and expertise. Read reports, reach out to any state agencies involved, talk to the lobbyists who work on those issues, and communicate with your allies. Make yourself an authority in a policy area—not a didactic know-it-all but someone who can provide answers and clarity when questions arise—and over time your colleagues will increasingly look to you as the expert in that area. Along the way, their respect for you as a lawmaker will grow as well.

A committee conversation with Senator Steve Conway. Negotiations in committee meetings are important as well as those on the floor. Notice how we are both shielding our conversation from being picked up by the many live microphones in committee or by the folks attending the hearing of the committee.

Identify who can help you make progress. You will have more time to devote to this undertaking in your first few years when less is demanded of you, and it will pay off in multiple ways as your legislative career develops. But in the short term, it will mean a lot of work and a lot of time. Prepare for some long days.

As you master your policy area, be mindful that expertise in itself is worthless if not wielded effectively. Depth of knowledge for its own sake can be a recipe for becoming a political gadfly, defined in one dictionary as: "A person who stimulates or annoys other people, especially by persistent criticism." While sometimes the gadfly's single-minded persistence is tolerated, I find the lawmaker who constantly "knows it all" will eventually be ignored.

Effective action on issues is critical to achieving legislative credibility and progress, but it is equally critical that these actions reflect your values. This passage from a marvelous poem by Langston Hughes captures perfectly, to me, our shared values as Americans:

Let America be the dream the dreamers dreamed—
Let it be that great strong land of love
Where never kings connive nor tyrants scheme
That any man be crushed by one above.[3]

We each have a set of values that keeps us centered and aligned with what we believe in and what we hold most dear. The most fundamental American value is probably freedom—freedom of speech, of association, of religion as codified in the First Amendment. Franklin Delano Roosevelt famously spoke of "four freedoms," including freedom from want and freedom from fear.[4] For some time now, many on the right have twisted this value by citing freedom of religion when imposing government action to ban or limit reproductive rights. It's a perverse example of hypocrisy, because true freedom is the absence of government interference with our rights as individuals.

Progressives can push back by insisting on the practice of freedom in its true sense on a host of fronts:

- Progressives can restore the value of FDR's freedom from fear— through our shared goals of eliminating hate speech, racial discrimination, sexual harassment, domestic abuse, and domestic terrorism.

- Progressives can restore the value of FDR's freedom from want through our goals of economic security, adequate human services, and solid labor and health standards.

- Progressives can restore the value of freedom of speech by redefining speech as communication and not campaign contributions, as the U.S. Supreme Court wrongly ruled in its Citizens United case when it eliminated campaign finance reform by interpreting corporate donations as speech.

- Progressives can restore the value of freedom of religion by insisting all religions be treated equally and without government favor, and that freedom of religion includes, as Thomas Jefferson held, freedom from religious preferences. "I am for freedom of religion, & against all maneuvers to bring about a legal ascendancy of one sect over another," Jefferson wrote in a letter to Elbridge Gerry on January 26, 1799.

- Progressives can restore the First Amendment value of freedom of association by requiring the free, unfettered ability of workers to organize into unions without interference. The freedom of association should also be invoked for protestors and demonstrations for racial justice.

Another key value for most progressives is opportunity. Equal opportunity goes hand in hand with equal treatment and is a fundamental standard for progressives. But while opportunity and treatment are often conflated, they mean two very different things. Equal treatment, for example, could mean that students who enter grade school are issued the same books and attend the same classes. But let's say one child is from a household that is experiencing homelessness, is headed by a single parent who is struggling to pay for rent, food, and childcare while working part-time jobs that pay poverty-level wages and no benefits, and whose life outside school is unstable and traumatizing. This child might receive equal treatment in school but will not experience equal opportunity because she is too tired, hungry, and distraught to pay attention in class. If we want that child to be able to succeed, it falls to government to create a level playing field so that she can enjoy an equal opportunity to learn and succeed and live as productive and healthy a life as her classmate.

Fair standards that create equal opportunity in both our social and economic lives are key goals for progressives. Equal opportunity for all, and not just the privileged, is fundamental. But opportunity must be more than just a word—it must be backed by affirmative actions that ensure true access to equal opportunity.

A third key value is security—not only economic security but physical and health security too. Progressives sometimes stumble in discussing how to keep people secure at all levels, in reassuring people that their safety and security is a top priority. But public security and safety is really the very first job of government. The public deserves security from domestic terrorists who would bomb government buildings, assassinate abortion providers, or terrorize others for real or perceived differences in race, gender, religious belief, or other characteristics. People who "work hard and play by the rules," as the cliché goes, deserve security from being devastated by unemployment or by financial shenanigans on the part of corporate profiteers and criminals. Anyone who has seen the devastation of medical bankruptcy knows well the irreplaceable need for health security. Hardworking families cannot succeed and thrive unless their freedom, opportunity, and security at every level can be assured by the makeup and enforcement of our laws.

Finally, progressives believe in the key value of hope—the natural antidote for fear. The right wing's unrelenting drumbeat of scary stereotypes and foreign and domestic threats has encouraged an attitude of fear and defensiveness that hinders positive progress. In contrast, President Obama's iconic 2008 campaign poster featuring one word, *HOPE*, partnered with his "Change We Can Believe In" campaign slogan, still stands as a fundamental progressive message. As progressives, it is paramount that we all work to "keep hope alive."[5]

KEY TAKEAWAYS

- The enthusiasm and energy of a new legislator needs the right channel and direction to become effective.
- Find your passion to create the avenue forward, and work to become the go-to member in that area.
- Apply your core values to advance your message about your issues inside and outside the legislature.
- Avoid becoming a gadfly, making comments so predictable that your colleagues might think, "There she goes again."

NOTES

1. George W. Scott, *A Majority of One: Legislative Life* (Seattle: Civitas Press, 2002), 18.

2. From "Casey at the Bat," a baseball poem first published in 1888 by the *San Francisco Chronicle* under the pen name of Phin, aka Lawrence Thayer.

3. "Let America Be America Again," a poem written in 1935 by American poet Langston Hughes, speaks of the American dream that never existed for the lower-class American and the freedom and equality that every immigrant hoped for but never received.

4. President Franklin Delano Roosevelt's 1941 annual Message to Congress outlined his concepts of freedom, now known as the "Four Freedoms Speech."

5. Obama For Change, *Change We Can Believe In: Barack Obama's Plan to Renew America's Promise* (London: Penguin Random House Books, 2008).

CHAPTER 14

Compromising Without Compromising Your Values

"Do we participate in a politics of cynicism or a politics of hope?"
—Barack Obama

All kinds of people, from hard-core ideologues to congenital deal makers, win seats in state legislatures. Ideologues often plant a flag and refuse to move it—and rarely win agreement. Deal makers constantly shift and twist to seal an agreement, giving up so much along the way that the eventual agreement doesn't achieve real change.

In 2017, the Legislature passed our state paid family and medical leave act into law. It had been a ten-year effort. This photo shows me in the wings of the House with Representative Mike Sells, then-chair of the House Labor Committee, watching the floor vote on the bill.

Every lawmaker knows her place between the ends of that spectrum. Self-awareness is the first requirement for successful, values-based negotiation. For newly elected women and people of color, being able to successfully negotiate is essential. Negotiations can play out well when you approach with a win-win, shared values approach. But you must know your own values going in.

Each person finds her own boundaries and tolerances. Working with colleagues who come from different backgrounds and cultures often informs and adds flexibility to those boundaries. Part of the legislative process that is so fascinating to me is the meeting of minds that occurs when two lawmakers from starkly different backgrounds and political persuasions find agreement.

I find clear, consistent values are my best guide when I'm considering a compromise. Negotiating on issues is easier when you have a clear vision of your values and can identify common values with the person or organization you are negotiating with. My key values are basic—fairness, freedom, family, security, and opportunity. These are broad terms that reflect values that are shared by many.

These concepts were put in action when we negotiated one of the best, if not *the* best, paid family and medical leave laws in the country in 2017. Shared values of family, fairness, and security all played a big part in successfully negotiating with the Republican majority and the business community. It was a breakthrough deal, and the strong bipartisan vote that cemented it was celebrated by all who had been at the table.

It's wise to use words people can agree with. Words are powerful, and smart political consultants test them in study groups.[1] For example, Lake Research Partners in 2019[2] found that:

- "Working people" is a more popular term than "workers."
- "Negotiating" is more positive than "bargaining."
- "Economic security" is more important than "economic growth."
- "Freedom" is very powerful, period.

Now put the values message together: "Working people should have the same freedom as CEOs to negotiate a fair return for their work." Voila!

These kinds of messaging exercises can open up routes to developing agreements, large and small.

Compromises can also be bargained on a limited, practical basis, with an acknowledgment that the compromise is short term or a transactional concession to move a bill forward out of committee. The potential danger in these incremental compromises is that you might find yourself on a slippery slope that can take you places you don't want to go. That's where bottom lines come in.

Any union member who has engaged in collective bargaining knows that compromises need to be made in order to reach an agreement. (The alternative is a strike that can create great hardship and peril for both sides.) Unions regularly and successfully negotiate contracts with wages, benefits, and working conditions on the table. Negotiators go to the table with bottom lines and topline goals—clear-headed parameters based on need and reality. Neither side walks away from the table without achieving some goals, but not all, and avoiding their bottom lines. Compromise is the oxygen of bargaining, whether the goal is a union contract or a piece of legislation.

Once you take office, you take on the responsibility of representation. Your job includes representing your constituents—some of whom did not vote for you. Your interest in advancing policies and values has to be balanced with your obligation to represent your constituents. Sometimes there's a conflict. While you can't in good conscience compromise your fundamental values or positions on issues, sometimes you can find a path forward that at least achieves some progress for all.

For example, as a strong advocate for working families and their unions, I faced a difficult conflict in my district, which contained the region's major international airport in the City of SeaTac. Constituents concerned about air pollution, noise, and property values opposed further expansion of the airport. At the same time, building a third runway would create more jobs and was strongly supported by labor. To effectively represent my constituents, I had to find a way to build credibility with those constituents who had not voted for me. I came out opposed to building the third runway because it would merely have been a stopgap measure that hurt tens of thousands of low-income constituents I represented.

Despite my opposition, the third runway was eventually built and, predictably, the increased air traffic has significantly degraded the environmental health of my district.[3] New evidence of ultrafine particulate pollutants from burning jet fuel has sharpened the debate. My approach was to propose and eventually pass legislation to find or build new commercial aviation facilities in the state to shift some of that traffic from SeaTac International Airport. It took a decade to pass, but organized labor supported the search for new airport capacity, so we were finally able to find agreement on the issue that was supported both by my constituents and by organized labor.

Other times, you just have to say "no." This can be particularly difficult for some people, often women, who may have been raised to always try and get to "yes" by making whatever accommodations it takes. But as uncomfortable as it can be to say "no," it can also be empowering. When the person across the negotiation table approaches my bottom line, I heed the lyric from the old Kenny Rogers song: "You've got to know when to hold 'em, know when to fold 'em, know when to walk away…"[4]

When you leave that table without an agreement, you need to do so with the resolve that there will always be another time and place when you'll return to that issue. And the next time they won't try to take you where you don't want to go. I keep a list of unfinished business that I return to when the time is right.

KEY TAKEAWAYS

- Fundamental progressive values can be expressed in words that most people will agree with.
- Use shared values as guideposts for negotiating.
- Identify your goals and bottom line before you get to the negotiating table.
- Don't be afraid to walk away if you can't reach a satisfactory agreement.

NOTES

1. Bernie Horn and Gloria Totten, *Voicing Our Values: A Message Guide for Policymakers and Advocates* (Public Leadership Institute, 2019), 15.

2. Lake Research Partners and Celinda Lake, "Advancing Bold Policy for America's Working Family," August 2019. Source: Anat Shenker-Osorio and ASO Communications, www.LakeResearch.com.

3. Sara Jean Green, "SeaTac's third runway set to open after years of delay," *Seattle Times*, September 26, 2008. https://www.seattletimes.com/seattle-news/sea-tacs-third-runway-set-to-open-after-years-of-delay/.

4. Don Schlitz, "The Gambler," 1976, recorded by Kenny Rogers.

CHAPTER 15

Money, Money, Money

*"I think members of the legislature, people who have to run for office, know the
connection between money and influence on what laws get passed."*
—Ruth Bader Ginsberg

Many potentially great women candidates for public office balk at the idea
of asking friends, family, or strangers for money for her campaign. The mere
thought makes them uncomfortable. Nevertheless, it is an absolutely necessary
task—something like scrubbing a stovetop or the bottom of a burned pan, a
skill one learns by doing. Having a consultant or campaign manager to manage
records and keep up morale during daily "call time" is a great help. But in the
beginning, you're often on your own. You learn how to ask for donations to
raise money or you don't win. And after you win, reality intrudes.

"Living on the salary of a citizen legislator is nearly impossible for most,"
noted first-time Senator Liz Lovelett. "Stagnation in compensation makes the
job untenable for people raising families and has made it largely a position for
wealthy people, retirees, or those with a working spouse."

To a successful candidate who raised tens of thousands of dollars to run a
winning campaign, it's something of a cold shower to discover the salary for the
seat you fought so hard to secure is pretty meager. The job has some perks, to
be sure, but the paycheck isn't one of them. As Larry Kenney, the iconoclastic
former president of the Washington state AFL-CIO noted, "Legislative pay
is lousy, the hours are long and abuse is endless, but you can get some good
candidates." He was right![1]

The vast majority of state legislatures are part-time institutions that pay part-
time salaries. Only ten states boast full-time legislatures that pay commensurate
compensation. The roots go back centuries—state legislatures accommodated
farmers and convened during the months when plowing and planting weren't
priorities. Other lawmakers who could afford to work part time included retirees
living off family wealth or pensions, public employees who could take unpaid
leave, thriving professionals, and self-employed businessmen.

When women began to run for office and win, they were usually married, with children who'd already grown. Most didn't have to support a family. Working people, people of color, and young people have always been in scarce supply in state legislatures. Many unions had bylaws prohibiting union staff from running for political office, possibly a legacy of efforts to prevent staff from becoming a challenge to a local union's leadership. But regardless of the reasons, in the end, this narrow demographic of office holders accounts for much of the conservative tilt of many state legislatures.

Legislative pay is always a political hot potato. The legislatures that pay the top five salaries are all full-time, ranging from $66,257 in Massachusetts to $110,459 in California. But only ten states have full-time legislatures. Salaries for part-time legislative service vary wildly and peculiarly. A legislator in Maine, for example, earns $14,074 in the first year of a biennial session and $9,982 in the second year, plus per diem. In Wisconsin, a lawmaker earns $52,999 a year plus per diem. Oregon pays $31,200 per year plus per diem. Washington's state legislature pays $52,766 per year plus per diem. All of these represent the rates of pay in 2020.[2]

It's also important to know that most legislative jobs provide comprehensive health care coverage and decent state pensions, provided you sign up for it.

Lawmakers report, on average, that they spend about 70 percent of their time on legislative work. It is hard to find a second job that requires only 25 to 30 percent of your time. Republican lawmakers often land part-time positions at rightwing nonprofits. Their nonprofit and business association network is a kind of farm team for them. Democrats haven't been able to build a similar system of sinecure for part-time legislators.

Per diem consists of daily pay for expenses such as traveling to and from the capital, renting lodging, and paying for meals. This too varies greatly between states, from zero per diem pay in New Jersey to $322 a day in Tennessee. Washington's per diem is $120 per day, Oregon's is $149 per day. And there's a caveat: IRS rules count per diem as income if you live less than fifty miles from the state Capitol. As I live forty-seven miles from the Capitol but need to also rent lodging during sessions, income taxes take a bite.

In between sessions, some members are keenly conscientious about keeping track of every little expense—whether it was the morning coffee or the quick gas fill-up—to report as a business expense. Some members serve on interim committees and task forces between legislative sessions that also may pay a per diem.

Since the Great Recession of 2009, many state legislatures eliminated or strictly limited travel to out-of-state conferences reimbursed by the state to one trip per year. Preapproved travel, hotel, and registration fees for one conference can be fully reimbursed by the Washington legislature. In-state travel is also reimbursable if the travel is for legislative business.

In addition, each legislative office is often accorded a budget for office expenses and for communications costs, such as stationery, business cards, and newsletter mailings. Office expenses can cover some travel costs, too, if the costs are within the office's annual budget, and they can be used to supplement partial scholarships to conferences. Some states have created generous office budgets as an offset to low salaries for legislators.

Well-heeled special-interest groups such as ALEC, a policy shop for conservative legislation, have regularly provided fully-funded "scholarships" to lovely resorts for legislators who support their agendas and sponsor their bills. I was able to arrange a far more modest $200 scholarship for a trip held in the oldest hotel in downtown Denver through a progressive policy group. Old hotels have their own charm, though.

About fifty years ago, the Olympia Stamp Act scandal exposed the practice of handing out rolls of stamps, to the tune of $8,000 in stamps for each Senate office.[3] The stamps could be used for office mail, political mail, or personal mail, and there was no accounting for it. This little racket came to light when a Republican state representative decided he'd prefer cash and redeemed $2,225 in stamps at his local post office. The issuing of stamps was prohibited soon after.

A legal financial device is sometimes employed by lawmakers who are vested into their legislative pensions. It is possible to increase the pension benefit significantly by resigning from the legislature and getting a higher paying state, county, or city job. For example, winning election to a full-time county commission position can pay a salary of $100,000 or more. Upon retirement, the monthly pension check will be increased significantly, reflecting the much higher salary of the last few years. That takes foresight and planning.

Then there's the campaign side of things.

Every state has different rules and laws regarding legislative expenses and campaign funds. In Washington state, if you have leftover campaign funds after a successful campaign, you can transfer those funds into what's called a surplus account, which can be used for certain legislative-related expenses such as travel to conferences or partisan political events. In 2012, I used surplus funds to attend the Democratic National Convention in North Carolina as a delegate to vote for President Obama's renomination and participate in convention events. It was a rich and unforgettable experience! More practical uses for young members include using surplus funds to pay for childcare costs while in session. Some male members have used such surplus funds to pay the dry-cleaning bills for the suits they wear during session.

You can also use surplus funds in Washington state to donate to your local legislative district, county party, or state party organizations, which is helpful for anyone with future political ambitions.[4] And if you feel generous, you can buy a table for a state-registered nonprofit organization's fundraiser with some of your surplus dollars. An out-of-state, nonregistered nonprofit does not qualify for your surplus dollars, however—you would need to use personal funds for that kind of donation. You cannot donate surplus funds directly to political action committees (PACs) or to candidates. Every state has different, often arcane and complicated rules, regarding political funds. Be sure to carefully abide by them.

Your own caucus will also expect you to donate surplus funds to your caucus campaign committee. These donations are tracked, and your standing in the caucus will likely be influenced by the level of your support for caucus campaign efforts. I confess to creating the surplus funds program in the Senate Democratic Campaign Committee when I was the campaign chair in 2004. It was a tradition I carried over from the House that had not been used previously in the Senate, and it became a very successful method to raise campaign funds for the caucus. Additional caucus expectations include fundraising and participating in caucus campaign events in years when you aren't running, so be sure to consider all these possibilities if you have a significant amount of leftover campaign dollars. Put enough in your surplus account so you will be able to fully participate and be considered "a player" by your legislative leadership. But keep enough for your own use, too.

The system favors those who run in safe districts and have lots of well-heeled donors because those candidates won't have to spend their donations to win their own races. Candidates in swing districts know they have to spend every dime they can raise, and maybe more, to win reelection. For them, the first reelection campaign is the hardest, often even harder than the original winning campaign, because they will be attacked for any controversial votes they cast while in office.

The opposition party will have been watching throughout your first term to track issues and voting records that they can use in hit pieces circulated during your reelection campaign. Your record on hot-button issues like raising taxes, abolishing the death penalty, limiting any kind of gun ownership, or requiring medically accurate sex education in public schools are all potential fodder for attack ads that progressive candidates who are up for their first reelection will have to withstand. Any candidate in a swing district should not spend their precious surplus funds on trips, political party events, or caucus campaign committees until after winning their first reelection by a comfortable margin.

Most lawmakers don't run for office for the money. Indeed, the low salaries and tough campaigns are deterrents for someone who needs to earn enough to support a family. Thousands of public servants, serving on everything from school boards to water districts, put in late hours for a nominal per diem and no salary at all. State legislators usually run because they are passionate about a cause and want to make a difference. And they can! They earn recognition and public appreciation and have the opportunity to make history and improve life for thousands of their constituents in many different ways.

Money isn't everything.

KEY TAKEAWAYS

- Be careful, especially in your first term, to set limits on spending so you don't find yourself with either personal or legislative budget problems.

- Decide how you want to deal with advocates and lobbyists who offer you meals, drinks, or invitations to social events.

- Know the rules. For instance, per diem is taxable income if you live less than fifty miles from the state Capitol.

- Conferences are valuable educational opportunities that are sometimes held in lovely places.

NOTES

1. https://ncsl.org/research/about-state-legislator-compensation.

2. www.Ballotpedia.org/comparison_of_state_legislative_salaries.

3. Senator George W. Scott. "Olympia Stamp Act," *Senate Journal Of The Thirty-Eighth Legislature Of The State Of Washington At Olympia, The State Capital,* January 14, 1963, 291.

4. Jason Bennett, campaign consultant, Argo Strategies, Seattle, 2020. On public disclosure rules regarding campaign and surplus funds.

CHAPTER 16

Staying in Tune

"Most of the successful people I've known are the ones who do more listening than talking."
—Bernard Baruch

It is an awesome honor to represent tens of thousands of constituents as an elected member of a state legislature. It is an exclusive club, and it can turn heads. The wild flurry of activities and obligations keeps members very busy, but do be careful—always take the time to meet with constituents and listen to them during session, just as you did when you knocked on their doors back home. Talk with them about education or health care or the environment, and listen hard when they tell you about property taxes or permit problems or the potholes in their streets.

These are real-life concerns, and don't forget—you asked your constituents to trust you to represent their concerns in the first place. These everyday matters impact their lives directly. Connect with them and stay connected through weekly communications during each legislative session. Make sure your office captures the names and email addresses and even phone numbers of all constituents who visit you during session. Keep a close tally on the big issues coming through the door from constituents, in person or by phone or by post card or by email. Monitor social media too.

Keep a separate tally by topic on the noise from all the others—non-constituents and interest groups—so that at a glance you can see where the money and pressure are coming from.

"All politics is local," was the best-known truism from Tip O'Neill, the long-time congressman from Boston who served as Speaker of the House for a full decade. State legislators soon realize that most of their constituents won't know their name. Despite the months of doorbelling, mailers, and campaign events, newly elected lawmakers aren't all that well known beyond their supporters. One critical job of every newly elected legislator is to get to know more of their constituents. It takes active, consistent outreach to connect and hear what's on the minds of those who didn't necessarily vote for you—or didn't vote at all.

"As a person of color, our districts don't have clear boundaries—anyone who was desperate to be heard and saw themselves in you became constituents," observed first-time Washington State Senator Joe Nguyen. "That's why I ran and that is what makes it all worth it—to fundamentally and forcefully change the political process to ensure our voices are uplifted."

Rally for educators and schools, 2015.

Rally in front of the Capitol building for a $15.00 minimum wage, 2016.

Senate gallery with students in conversation with Representative Shay Schual-Berke, 2004.

During normal (non-pandemic) sessions, advocates often travel to Olympia, the Washington state capital, to rally for their causes. They typically ask legislators who support them to join their events.

Before email, most communication during a legislative session was by letter or phone. The legislative toll-free hotline was a major conduit prior to email. Now, with huge numbers of emails every session, it is an increasing challenge for lawmakers to find time to read and respond individually.[1] Legislative assistants, session aides, and interns can help by responding to the multiple form letter emails that come in on controversial topics with a detailed reply you that have preapproved.

A bill in 2020, for instance, mandated that all schools provide age-appropriate comprehensive sexual health education and generated thousands of emails from opponents and hundreds from supporters.[2] But whoever the constituent is who contacts you during session, it's a good idea to provide a prompt thank-you and response. It's a helluva lot of work, and sometimes the responses have to be a standard template, but not responding is a serious mistake. Personal responses are always best, although in the press of a busy session, a personal reply can be difficult bordering on impossible. New members are wise to carve out an hour or two of evening time to make phone calls and write emails to constituents. Underestimate the importance of individualized communications at your risk.

About halfway through session, on the weekend after the deadline for bills to have passed over to the other chamber, many members arrange to hold town hall meetings back home to take the temperature of the district and to discuss issues and bills they've been focused on in session. New members sometimes try to do multiple town halls in different communities during that weekend. Your office and communications staff can provide or prepare handouts, talking points, and bill reports to help explain key issues.

Managing your office communications is hard work—with dozens of constituents who come in person on an organized lobby day, or a deluge of emails on the hot topic of the day, or drop-ins from back home, or countless lobbyists asking for fifteen-minute meetings. Regular email updates, along with Facebook posts or live streaming, videos and printed pre- and post-session legislative reports, news releases, and op-ed columns are the job of your PIO (public information officer) or communications staff person. In my view, nearly all communications should be focused on what you are doing for your district and your constituents. That is your touchstone for "all politics is local."

After a legislative session ends, typical outreach may include a telephone town hall meeting where constituents can call in or a predictive dialer calls out to constituents in your district. In-person town halls are standard practice for after-session roundups. In districts that encompass multiple cities, members might hold two or three in-person town hall meetings in a day. These require a considerable amount of coordination. Zoom and Facebook Live events are increasingly popular, but no one knows if those who participate are constituents or not, and there's no practical system for possible follow-up contact.

My first legislative assistant recalls the nightmare of my first town hall meeting attracting a grand total of a single constituent![3] Another time, we were overrun after we decided to offer a free slice of pie from a popular local café—so many folks showed up that we had to move the town hall meeting from the café to the city hall, along with the pies. What a mess! If you are able to join forces with your district seatmates from the other chamber to jointly host a town hall meeting, the tough work of outreach and coordination can be spread across more staff. These events are lots of work and staff does most of it, so be sure to make known your appreciation and gratitude for their great work.

Constituent outreach can also invite pitfalls, however well intended. I was told a former senator was scolded by the state ethics committee for writing personal notes on her Senate note cards to people who were listed in her local newspaper as winning an award or suffering a setback. In today's legislature, the line between legislative purpose and non-legislative matters is firm—communications from legislators and their offices must be limited to legislative matters.

Coming home to your district after spending months of intense effort in a legislative session can feel disconcerting sometimes. Give yourself some time to decompress and reconnect. As one of my favorite writers, Bill Bryson, observed: "Coming back to your native land after an absence of many years is a surprisingly unsettling business, a little like waking from a long coma. Time, you discover, has wrought changes that leave you feeling mildly foolish and out of touch."[4]

Some legislative sessions that are full of sharp debates and tough floor fights can feel like you've been in a different world. It's always nice to get home again.

The legislative interim—the months between legislative sessions—is a time for you to increase your presence. Some members hold regular hours at local coffee shops to meet with folks. It's also important to show up at just about every event you can get to in your district. From a chamber of commerce meeting to a local union meeting to a ribbon-cutting for a new business or a groundbreaking for a new health clinic, all are opportunities that should not be overlooked by new lawmakers.

Another truism of local politics: 90 percent of the job is just showing up. And listening.

Nowhere is this more evident than when it comes to casework, which is a social worker's term that is quite appropriate—and also one of the heartaches and joys of legislative life.

When constituents don't know where to turn, they frequently contact your legislative office—by phone or email, or even when they see you at the grocery store. The problem is often an urgent matter that involves a dispute or disagreement with a state agency.

In Washington state, our legislative assistants become real experts in figuring out ways to help, sometimes by referring them to community resources, sometimes by connecting their complaint to an agency liaison. But you might need to intervene directly as well, with either the constituent or the agency. The satisfaction from fixing a problem for a constituent is a marvelous feeling, for both you and your staff. Especially when your party is in in the minority, finding solutions for a constituent's problem gives special meaning to the word *representative*. But at times, a deluge can almost overwhelm you.

When the sweeping economic shutdown from the 2020 COVID-19 pandemic hit, the number of unemployment insurance claims to our state Employment Security Department went from an average of 5,000 a week to 500,000 a week. There was simply no way for a staff designed to handle 5,000 claims a week to suddenly process a more-than-thousand-fold increase in claims, and hiring and training additional staff added agonizing weeks to the process.

To make things worse, it turned out several thousand of those claims were fraudulent, organized by a criminal network that targeted our program because we were the fastest to implement the increased federal benefits first, as we knew how desperately people needed help. When the fraudsters were detected, the agency froze tens of thousands of suspicious claims in order to confirm that applications were legitimate before releasing funds. Meanwhile, our offices were inundated with calls and emails from constituents who hadn't received unemployment checks. They couldn't pay their bills or their rent or even buy food for their children. Every office heard from dozens of constituents every day, and their pleas were heartbreaking. Many emails were sent in the early morning hours, which told me the senders were at their wits end trying to find help.

We struggled with the agency and with our constituents to build a bridge to resolve confirmation issues ranging from identity to employers to hours worked. It was horrible for our staff, and we felt powerless to fix the problems.

This went on for nearly ten weeks, but finally the claims were cleared and the complaints ebbed to a trickle. Hearing back from so many constituents whom we helped made it one of the most satisfying casework projects I ever experienced.

Legislative work can be emotionally draining, and it can be wildly exhilarating—but it is never dull.

KEY TAKEAWAYS

- Keep your ears to the ground to hear what your constituents, and non-constituents, are most concerned about.

- Use every possible available tool to communicate to your constituents during session and after session.

- Your constituents won't know what you are fighting for unless you tell them.

- When not in session, attend as many local events as you possibly can.

NOTES

1. In 2020 my office received approximately 5,000 emails from constituents, all needing a response, during the short sixty-day session. In longer biennial sessions, the number can easily triple.

2. SB 5395, introduced in 2019 and signed into law in 2020, provides for age-appropriate, comprehensive sex education to be taught in all public schools, with a parental opt-out option.

3. Sue Evans, Facebook message to author, April 2020.

4. Bill Bryson, *I'm A Stranger Here Myself: Notes on Returning to America after Twenty Years Away*, New York: Broadway Books, 1999, p. 2.

CHAPTER 17

Watch Your Back and Keep Score

"African Americans have always known a little bit of paranoia is healthy for us."
—U.S. Representative Cynthia McKinney

All legislators are paranoid. Some just a little, others see enemies everywhere. As Joseph Heller said, "Just because you're paranoid doesn't mean they aren't after you."[1]

The truth is lawmakers have good reason to be paranoid. Getting a bill passed means running a seemingly endless gauntlet. The first hurdle comes after you introduce your bill—it must be referred to a committee to be heard, and what might seem to be the most obvious committee for your bill isn't necessarily where it will be sent. Depending on the chair and the members of a given committee, that committee might welcome your bill or be openly hostile—and hostility takes many forms. An unfriendly chair might refuse to hear the bill altogether. Or if it is heard, anyone on the committee may move to amend it—and the amendment might be a benign gesture to improve the bill, or it may be an opposing effort to gut it. If your bill passes out of committee relatively intact, there's no guarantee it will be pulled to the floor for a vote of the full Senate. And should it make it to the floor, anyone in the Senate may again move to amend it for better or worse. But let's say the bill gets passed by the Senate pretty much in its intended form. Then the whole process starts over, in the House, from being referred to committee on forward. But where forty-eight colleagues had the opportunity to oppose or amend your bill in the Senate, there are ninety-eight legislators in the House with the same opportunity. And even if they didn't have issues with your bill in the first place, they are constantly being lobbied by people paid to block your bill from being passed. There may be no shortage of people motivated to kill your bill, often hiding their intentions until the last minute. In that light, paranoia isn't so much a failing as a tenet of survival.

In some ways, the legislature can seem like a high school, with a lot of cliques and caucuses and status markers, like who has the best office or parking space. In fact, a lot of those perks come as a matter of seniority, where longevity—unlike in pop culture or corporate culture—is actually rewarded.

I never liked high school, and I am not interested in perks. I have outlasted a lot of other legislators, and seniority does have its privileges, which I thoroughly enjoy. I'm old enough now to be allowed some "cranky old woman" space, which I also thoroughly enjoy. But I am still paranoid enough to know that the back-slapping and friendly laughs to your face can soon be followed by a metaphorical shiv in your back.

When I was a reporter, I learned how to ingratiate myself with individuals and sources to get a good quote or important fact. It wasn't authentic friendship, just friendly wheedling—a device to get a story. Lobbyists and colleagues employ that same kind of friendly socializing to get a vote. It's part of their game.

Sometimes that game gets rough. My advice is to be careful and watchful, and don't fully trust anyone who hasn't proved their trustworthiness to you in some real and authentic way. Rely on the fundamental legislative currency that is as good as gold: credibility and trustworthiness, for yourself as well as others.

Opposition is not the same as some of the oddly personal sense of insult or long-simmering grudge that some legislators harbor. I have had a couple of these experiences and they are not pleasant; they can be infuriating. Personally, I find them fundamentally puzzling. One came from a member with a powerful political supporter. She was a short-serving member who famously led our caucus over the cliff with political defeats and faceplants on the floor. When she left, no one cared. Few members are actually downright mean, but some have issues. Another member was so arrogant and rude he should have been charged with harassment—but he didn't survive his first reelection effort. I recall one member with serious insecurity issues who occasionally reacted with angry venom. The legislature isn't really like most other workplaces—outsized egos, large personalities, and aggressive scheming are part and parcel of political life.

One more piece of advice: treat your staff with respect and professional courtesy. They are not your personal servants or political water carriers. I have seen many legislators breach the standards of professionalism by becoming overly friendly or imperious and demanding. All legislative staff have a big job to do—to help members succeed. Good staff support is the secret behind every legislative success. From your office staff to caucus staff to committee staff and chamber staff, appreciation for the work they do should be part of your workplace ethos.

Don't overlook the potential for lobbyists to spread a rumor or plant misinformation. Skilled lobbyists don't often get personal with members, but they have clients who want them to kill bills and one of those bills might be a bill you want to move. Some lobbyists you can trust, some you can't. The better lobbyists learn the importance of trustworthiness early on and don't try to mislead you. Some never figure that out.

If your priority bill suddenly dies an unnatural death, start asking questions about what the hell happened. Talk to colleagues, talk to staff, talk to lobbyists, talk to your allies. Figure out who stabbed you in the back. You don't need to make a public scene or confront the culprit. A few strong words in the "privacy" of your office will be heard around the chamber. A good memory is also useful, as articulated best by Robert F. Kennedy: "Don't get mad, get even."

Ninety percent of the time, colleagues, lobbyists, and staff will treat you honestly and fairly. My recommendation is to focus on the 90 percent—don't nurse your grievances, move forward. As for the other 10 percent—watch your back, develop a long memory, and keep score.

Keeping a little book on who has done, or has not done, what you want is the old-fashioned pol's version of keeping score. It's been reported that House Speaker Nancy Pelosi's job when her father was mayor of Baltimore was to fill out his little book of favorites.[2] When in power, the Clintons were famously known for keeping track of friends, and keeping them close—the FOB, or Friends of Bill, was an exclusive clique.

When you come to the legislature as a newly elected state lawmaker, you are eager, excited, and earnest. But you should also be watchful and observant. Some members have a clear sense of purpose and a reputation for getting things done. Others may be malleable and will go along to get along. Some bring large personalities with noise and presence but have no real impact. A few are loners who march to their own drums, usually at a predictable beat. Some may be visionaries with firm goals who take practical steps with long-term strategies.

But regardless of who you are, the legislative leaders and leadership team members will hold the levers of power with which to grant your legislative initiatives life or death.

Once you take the measure of your colleagues, you will figure out how to work with them—or around them. You will soon develop a mental inventory of who helps and who undermines what you hope to achieve. It's important to know who you can trust and rely on. And it's just as important to reach beyond those you can rely on to build bridges for the future. Keeping score must be part of your analysis and strategy.

A transactional quid pro quo can also be useful. For example, in the Rules Committee, if you need a bill pulled to the floor, you can make an agreement with another Rules member to pull a bill they want as long as they pull your bill. This is a classic, simple this-for-that transaction. But it can become complicated by deals on amendments or floor strategy. Just remember, if your agreement goes sideways for some reason, be sure to keep score. You must know who you can trust and who you can't.

Beware, however—this process can become destructive if it becomes a descent into retribution or pure payback. If someone betrays your trust and actively undercuts your efforts, it's natural to get angry and upset. But plotting revenge is foolish and counterproductive. Watch and wait, and the time will come when that individual who treated you poorly will need your vote. Then you can choose whether to be Lady Bountiful, and forgive and forget, or take sweet revenge. In the long days of the legislature, there always comes a time.

So be patient and have a long memory.

KEY TAKEAWAYS

- Credibility and trustworthiness are the keys of the legislature.
- Don't forget who failed or betrayed you.
- If you don't know who killed your bill, ask around—your questions will reverberate.
- Despite the despicable acts of a few, focus on the generous and positive acts of all the rest.

NOTES

1. Quote: https://www.goodreads.com/quotes/665107-just-because-you-re-paranoid-doesn-t-mean-they-aren-t-after-you.

2. Stephanie Salmon, "10 Things You Didn't Know About Nancy Pelosi," *US News and World Report*, November 7, 2016. https://www.usnews.com/news/articles/2006/11/07/10-things-you-didnt-know-about-nancy-pelosi.

CHAPTER 18

Gucci Loafers

"If you can't eat their food and drink their wine and vote against them, you shouldn't be in the political Arena."
—Governor Dan Evans[1]

Women have been working as lobbyists in the Washington State Legislature for decades, but—surprise!—their path has been more difficult than men's. Women lobbyists have had to create their own space and credibility, and they've been successful.

Forty years ago the Third House, as the lobbying corps calls itself, hosted an annual golf tournament for members of the legislature. All of the lobbyists were men, and so were the members who were invited to the tournament, which was called the Fly Open. This monopoly ended when women began working as lobbyists and decided to hold their own golf tournament. They called it the Double Cup, a wry joke and jab, and it's been going on for years as a way to socialize and enjoy some silly fun.

Lobbyists are actually what you might consider the professional lawmakers, while the elected lawmakers are usually the amateurs as their average stay in the state capitols is relatively short. Because lobbyists return year after year and grow deep roots, they develop considerable knowledge and solid relationships with legislative staff and lawmakers—at least the good lobbyists do. Lobbyists will work hard to persuade you to support their client's view. You may share that view already, but my advice is: don't be an easy mark. Unless you already know the lobbyist extremely well, make her work for your vote. Hold your opinions close until you have the full picture and want the lobbyist to just go away and leave you alone.

Many lobbyists are former lawmakers or legislative staff. Private-sector lobbyists dress well and make far more money than legislators. They wear nicer shoes, drive better cars, and dine well. We may know how to spell *Gucci*, but they know what it's like to wear it. Public-sector and public-interest lobbyists, by contrast, are constrained by modest budgets and a lack of expense accounts, in keeping with the leaner means of their clients. They're driven by the big cause, not the big paycheck. But both kinds of lobbyists are in it to win it, and they play hard.

The original "Ulcer Gulch," circa 1990s, before cell phones, text messages, and email, where the lobbyists hobnob with each other and try to get some face time with lawmakers.

One big reason why term limits for legislators are so dangerous is that the lobbyists never seem to leave. Legislators who stick around for only a few years hardly get to know their way around, while lobbyists boast long years of expertise. It took me years to figure out where the Rules Committee room was and to appreciate the committee's tremendous importance. Learning who gets what and why takes a very long time to understand if you don't have a mentor to advise you. Hence the lobbyists' outsized role as the unelected Third House of the legislature; their vast institutional knowledge and experience gives them a tremendous advantage over many a fledgling legislator learning the ropes. It's a sobering reality that lobbyists often know what will happen with an issue or a bill before lawmakers or staff know, or whether the legislative calendar will extend into a special session. For both rumors and insider tips, the lobbyists' grapevine is extraordinary. I'd swear those marble walls have ears.

There was a time, not so long ago, when lobbyists hosted lawmakers to dinner three or four nights a week, when poker games and drinking and partying were common. That may still be the norm for some state legislatures. In any case, it certainly made a legislative session a lot more fun for some and provided a relief valve for others, but now those days are largely gone. In Washington state, any hosted event costing more than fifty dollars per lawmaker must be reported as a public record and a lawmaker can accept no more than twelve dinners per year. In place of complimentary bottles of booze and other gifts, a nice bouquet of flowers is about the limit these days. The institutions have adopted a sober and strait-laced mien. You can still find booze on campus, and plenty of lawmakers find ways to let their hair down after a high-pressure day, but the era of lobbyists arriving the first day of session with car trunks full of booze to dole out to members' offices is a relic of the past. But that past was abundant with colorful incidents that sometimes led to scandal.

Lobbyists are not evil people. But they are hired guns. One lobbyist I know refers to himself and his colleagues as "paid friends." They might represent a business, a union, or some kind of profession or association. Their clients' goals may be private-sector profit or public good, or even some mix of both. Some lobbyists work on contract and handle many different clients, sometimes related, often not. Sometimes they even represent clients with opposing interests, but they generally observe an unwritten code of ethics to avoid client conflicts. Most of all, they love to gossip about each other—and anyone else in the Capitol universe.

The most important credential lobbyists have is their credibility. If you cannot trust a lobbyist to tell you the truth and to be an honest broker with the information known to them, you can't afford to waste your time meeting with them. Conversely, your credibility will also be judged by the Third House, and if you tell a lobbyist one thing but do another, your own credibility will be at risk.

That credibility can be jeopardized in other ways, such as when a lobbyist was seen making out with a married legislator by the highly public Tivoli Fountain on the Capitol Campus, or when a lobbyist with a reputation for bedding lawmakers was finally caught by security in a tryst with a member in a work room. That lobbyist's rationale: she matter-of-factly told people her job was "to get the men in the room"—a reference that in her case acquired a double meaning. Another lobbyist, frustrated by a committee chair's resistance to his exertions, made a loud and vulgar show of sticking pins in various anatomical parts of a voodoo doll he identified to his colleagues as the chair in question—in the highly visible lobby of a public building on campus. The lobbyists' subsequent apologies to the lawmaker did little to undo the damage to his client and, more lastingly, to his professional standing. While unquestionably memorable, these colorful missteps are far more the exception than the rule. Regardless of their clients' positions, the majority of lobbyists conduct themselves responsibly and professionally.

Leadership of every caucus meets with big-interest-group lobbyists, sometimes in a shared setting, discussing concerns and promoting their favorite bills. Business has its meeting. Labor has its meeting. Tribes have their meetings. Committee chairs hold group and individual meetings with interest groups over policy—health care, education, transportation, corrections, environment, labor, economic development, human services—and all get their turn to provide input in the push and pull of the legislative session. It is all about information sharing and a show of respect. But the real deals get done in smaller venues.

Sometimes the real deals are corrupt, and most of those cases typically involve lobbyists, legislative leadership, and payoffs.

In July 2020, the FBI raided the office of Ohio's Speaker of the House, Larry Householder, and arrested him and four associates on charges of bribery. Householder was accused of making a deal to pass legislation providing a billion-dollar subsidy, paid for by electric rate payers, to prop up two nuclear plants and eliminate renewable energy incentives—with Householder in line for a $60 million payoff. One of Ohio's best-connected lobbyists was also arrested.[2]

In 2018, the New York state legislature was rocked when both the State Assembly Speaker and the Senate Majority Leader were convicted in separate, unrelated cases of corruption.[3]

In 1980, a double-whammy corruption scandal hit the Washington State Legislature when both the House Speaker and Senate Majority Leader were arrested and convicted in an FBI sting known as "GamScam" involving legalized gambling.[4]

In 1975, one of the most colorful characters in Washington legislative history was found not guilty despite his admission of a lucrative quid pro quo with a waste management company. In a stern admonishment to Senate Majority Leader Augie Mardesich after the not guilty verdict was rendered, federal judge Charles Renfrew said, "Mr. Mardesich, I think you are a very fortunate man indeed.... There was sufficient evidence...on which a jury could have found you guilty on both counts." This was after the top officer of the waste management company, Bayside Disposal, had told the court, "They did a job for me and I paid them."

One very special interest that seems to wield inordinate influence and the deepest of pockets to pay lobbyists is the pharmaceutical industry, aka Big Pharma. The chief pharma lobbyist mobilized uncommonly fierce opposition when Representative Eileen Cody introduced legislation some years ago to establish a preferred drug list for the Medicaid program. The lobbyist was seen handing out individual contracts to a line of lobbyists standing at the sundial that separates the House and Senate office buildings. As the contract lobbyists signed up, dozens of different drug companies lined up to fight the bill. Despite that coordinated opposition, however, Representative Cody's bill passed into law. "That was quite a fight," she said afterward. "We did get the bill passed, and it has saved the state millions of dollars!"

I've always been amazed at the number of lobbyists Big Pharma can hire to kill a bill. When we worked on a prescription drug transparency bill a few years ago, the drug manufacturers were not the only opponents. There were so many middlemen, each taking their bites, that it was akin to the infamous "death by a thousand cuts." There were pharmacy benefit managers, pharmacists and drug stores, wholesale drug distributors—the list went on and on. The industry can present an amazing, orchestrated opposition that deploys lobbyists at multiple levels and in every crevice. And they almost always are able to kill bills, neuter them, or, at the very least, water them down. In the end, they were able to nearly eliminate the public release of any drug price increase data in the drug-price transparency bill that eventually passed three years later.

Political action committees and campaigns can become tangled up when lobbyists in the legislature also are a source for campaign contributions. The consequences of a bad vote may well mean a loss of a future campaign donation. The soundest advice to lawmakers is to never allow the implied or explicit threat to influence you.

More than a decade ago, a state senator who chaired a key committee received an email that alarmed her. She felt it was blatantly political and inappropriate, so she forwarded it to the Senate Majority Leader. The letter, written by a labor lobbyist, questioned the depth of the party's support for labor priorities and said the Democratic campaign committees might expect "not another dime from labor" until or unless The Worker Privacy Act was passed and signed into law by the Governor. The email was shared with the House Speaker and the Governor, who reportedly asked the State Patrol to investigate. Though the State Patrol found nothing criminal about the email, the Governor killed the bill, saying the email had raised "serious legal and ethical questions." The entire kerfuffle created a deep rift and bad feelings that lingered for years. During that time, the House and Senate caucus campaign committees were boycotted by most of labor. In the next campaign cycle, the Democrats lost the Senate majority. For six years, the Democratic House would pass progressive bills, only to see them come over to the Senate to die. From my perspective, it was painful and ultimately caused more harm than good.

Of course, if we had public financing for campaigns, these kinds of misunderstandings and confrontations would not happen in the first place. The corrupting power of money in politics is a constant threat that must be guarded against. And your best defense rests in your own good sense to avoid both threats and temptations.

In some states, there's a vivid dividing line between legislative business and campaign business. In Washington state, when a lobbyist asks for an "off campus" meeting, that is code language for requesting a political conversation about campaign ramifications. Most lobbyists know not to mix campaign conversations with the business of legislating; when that line gets crossed, complications arise, and it's never pretty. My advice: don't go there during session.

The public disclosure of campaign contributions, political action committees, and lobbyists and their employers can shed sunshine on much of the business of lobbying. The Washington State Public Disclosure Commission maintains the registration of lobbyists. There's lots of information about who works for what outfit and how much they're paid. And the Third House actually has its own website for new member sign-ups! Pharmaceutical companies and Pharma, the industry trade association, regularly appear at the top tier of the number of lobbyists hired and who are paid very well. The PDC lobbyist reports invariably make very interesting reading. Every state handles this puzzle differently, but the key for now is to keep your eyes open and follow the money.

Lobbyists can be helpful to lawmakers, or they can prove diabolical. They have their own culture and clients, and although they'll be unfailingly friendly and encouraging, it's safest to take anything they tell you with a grain of salt. Someone once said, "Trust, but verify," and that isn't a bad idea when it comes to lobbyists—even those you've known for years.[5]

KEY TAKEAWAYS

- Learn which lobbyists you can trust and which ones you can't as you watch what they say and do to you and to others.
- Be very careful not to mix campaign activities and legislative activities by drawing your own bright line between them.
- A good lobbyist can be very helpful as you work to pass legislation.
- A good lobbyist can also kill your bill.

NOTES

1. The Evans quote is an adaptation of a quote from longtime California Speaker Jesse Unruh, who famously said, "If you can't take their money, eat their food, drink their booze, screw their women and vote against them, you don't belong here." *Tacoma News Tribune*, March 25, 1975, 247.

2. Associated Press: Julie Carr Smyth, John Seewer, "Ohio House Speaker Arrested in $60M bribery case," July 22, 2020.

3. Brendan Pierson, "Ex-NY Senate Leader Gets Prison in Federal Corruption Case," *Reuters*, October 24, 2018: "Dean Skelos was sentenced on Wednesday to four years and three months in prison on federal corruption charges, including soliciting bribe, and defrauding the public." Jon Campbell, *Democrat & Chronicle*, July 20, 2018: "Silver, a Manhattan Democrat, was one of the most powerful people in New York government during his two-decade tenure as Speaker of the Assembly, which ended when he was indicted in 2015."

4. "GamScam was one of the most well-known scandals to hit Washington state politics. In 1980, two powerful Democrats, co-House Speaker John Bagnariol and Senate Majority Leader Gordon Walgren, were charged after an FBI sting caught them agreeing to allow gambling in the state in exchange for part of the profits." Kit Oldham, www.HistoryLink.org, March 3, 2008.

5. Nina Porzucki, "Suzanne Massie taught President Ronald Reagan this important Russian phrase: 'Trust, but verify,'" *The World*, March 7, 2014. Massie told the president: "You know the Russians often like to talk in proverbs and there's one that might be useful.... You're an actor, you can learn it in a minute: 'Trust, but verify.'" https://theworld.org/stories/2014-03-07/suzanne-massie-taught-president-ronald-reagan-important-russian-phrase-trust.

CHAPTER 19

You Can Call Me Madam President

"To every little girl who dreams big:
Yes, you can be anything you want—even president."
—Hillary Clinton

I was elected by my Senate colleagues to serve as President Pro Tempore for the January 2018 legislative session after Democrats took back the majority by one seat in a 2017 special election. President Pro Tempore is generally perceived as a largely honorary position—and I truly am honored to hold it—but it is also critical to the smooth operation of the Senate.

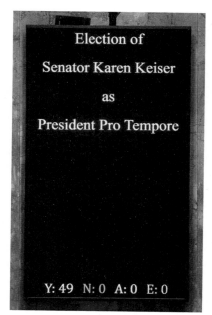

The President Pro Tempore presides over Senate floor action when the Lieutenant Governor—whose primary responsibility in Washington state is the dual role of Senate President—is temporarily serving as Governor or is otherwise unavailable due to scheduling conflicts.[1] When Governor Jay Inslee decided to run for President in 2019, for instance, he traveled out of state for several days during the many weeks we were in session. That year I presided on the Senate floor on thirty-two days, which I think may have set a record for a year with no special sessions.

Presiding brings an entirely new perspective to the legislative process. Colleagues I normally address by their first names must suddenly be addressed by their formal titles. I, in

Election of

Senator Karen Keiser

as

President Pro Tempore

Y: 49 N: 0 A: 0 E: 0

The announcement of my unanimous election to President Pro Tempore.

turn, am no longer "Karen" or even "Senator Keiser" to my colleagues but "Madam President" when commanding the rostrum. It also increases the propensity for verbal slips.

When the Lieutenant Governor presides, it's not uncommon for a House member-turned-Senator to address him as "Mr. Speaker" from habit instead of "Mr. President," which never fails to trigger friendly chiding from colleagues on the floor. But when I preside, I've been called everything from "Mr. President" to "Madam Speaker" to "Madam Chair," sometimes multiple times by a single flustered senator in a single floor speech. It's understandable when you consider that a senator may be overly focused on making a correct parliamentary motion, but that doesn't make the fumble any less comical—and the laughter that erupts on the floor invariably provides welcome relief from tense or unusually long floor action.

Presiding at the podium during a little comic relief, 2018.

Watching the floor from the podium, as members work their bills and gather their votes, can reveal who is likely to get a bill passed. Or you see some members wander aimlessly, chatting and socializing and forgetting they have a bill to move on the floor calendar. It's never a static picture, and it's always insightful.

Every biennial session in the Washington State Legislature, each member receives a little red book called the Legislative Manual. It is wise to read the section dealing with the permanent rules of the body. For example, Rule 28 of the Permanent Rules of the House set forth that "Smoking of cigarettes, pipes or cigars shall not be permitted." This is a legacy of former Representative Georgette Valle, who fought for years beginning in 1973 to prohibit smoking in public places including the floors of the House and Senate. At one point, Representative Valle persuaded the state Board of Health to adopt a rule and passed a floor resolution to end smoking in the state Capitol, including a requirement for *No Smoking* signs. Hearing through the grapevine that the Transportation Commission intended to ignore the new rule, Representative Valle called on Attorney General Kenneth Eikenberry to enforce it, and Representative Valle went to the commission's next meeting to check for herself. "I returned to the high-ceilinged room," she recalled later, "and saw a tiny, tiny 'No Smoking' sign about 25 feet up on the wall. I could hardly see the sign. I laughed and left the meeting." But she got the last laugh—in 1985 the Washington Indoor Clean Air Act became law and applied to all public places, including the Capitol.

In the Permanent Rules of the Senate, Rule 25 is simple and inflexible: "No bill shall embrace more than one subject and that shall be expressed in the title." This rule explains why so many bills have long, technical titles referencing several sections of underlying law. It can get tricky.

During floor session, bill action may be perfunctory and routine, or it can invoke high drama. It can also provide for unintended moments of humor, as when I recognize a member by their more familiar first name, once addressing Senator Manka Dhingra instead as "Senator Manka." Oops!

I am no expert parliamentarian. But legislatures, unions, and countless other organizations follow parliamentary procedures in their meetings for good reason. Such procedures ensure the minority has legal standing and the opportunity to voice its views. The formal dialogue and procedures also discourage personal attacks and even fisticuffs. Keeping good order on the floor is an art in itself. Under the rules, the president "shall preserve order and decorum and in case of any disturbance or disorderly conduct...shall order the sergeant at arms to suppress the same and may order the arrest...."[2]

Robert's Rules of Order is the chief parliamentary bible; an additional text known as Reed's Rules is also in use in the Washington State Legislature and in other state bodies. Some states also use Mason's and Jefferson's rules. The Floor Leader is the member who makes the motions for bills on First Reading, where they are assigned to committees after introduction. The presiding officer responds: "Hearing no objection, so ordered." And the gavel drops. Only a small percentage of bills referred to committee will survive the arduous legislative gauntlet and make it to a floor calendar, where they can be brought back up on the floor for Second Reading. During Second Reading, bills are subject to amendment on the floor. Controversial bills may draw scores of amendments in an effort to kill the bill (or other bills) by simply running out the clock or by passing an amendment that weakens or emasculates the bill. A glance at the increased audience in the Senate gallery can give a clue to anyone who looks to anticipate what kind of floor fight is coming.

As President Pro Tempore, I have presided over hours-long amendment battles, with plenty of motions and arguments and objections to rule on. And though the position is generally viewed as honorary, the skill level of the President Pro Tempore can mean the difference between crisp, orderly floor action or meandering, raucous debate that wastes hours. At any time, a loud voice may call out, "I object," creating a stir and requiring the presiding officer to determine the merits of the objection. As President Pro Tempore, you no longer represent your caucus but the larger institution of the full Senate—and sometimes you have to rule against your own personal preference. The added responsibility of preserving the integrity of the institution and the credibility of one's rulings on challenges to procedures can mean conflict and consternation. But you assume that responsibility when you are elected with the vote of all the members, not only the members of your own caucus. It may sound arcane, but there are real and lasting ramifications.

Presiding as President Pro Tempore, 2018.

I was presiding when a marijuana bill was brought forward that would have created a system of labor representation and allowed out-of-state investors. I supported the bill and had voted for it in committee. But the opposition objected based on the "two-subject" rule, meaning a bill must contain only one subject. I stepped away from the podium to consult with the caucus attorneys, who found the objection legitimate. I ruled in favor of the objection, effectively killing the bill. I could have used my authority to rule against the objection and save the bill that day, but it would have been killed in other ways, and—more importantly—I would have called into question the impartiality of the Senate President. It was a painful day, but I had no choice. And the sponsor of the bill learned a painful lesson: remember Rule 25!

When the bill on the floor is moved to Third Reading, the time for amendments is closed, and final floor speeches commence. Then the vote is called. Good floor management and coordination avoids failure, as it is a rare bill that will get to Third Reading without a solid vote count. The unwritten rule that is operational in floor action for the majority caucus is "the rule of no surprises." No majority leader wants to be surprised with a bad vote count, and there will be consequences if it happens on an important bill. The minority caucus often seeks to pull a surprise on the floor, but since the marble walls seem to have ears and everyone is listening, it is rare indeed for a real surprise to occur.

Under the permanent rules of the Senate, the President Pro Tempore "shall have all the powers and authority, and shall discharge all the duties of lieutenant governor acting as president during the lieutenant governor's absence." It sounds important—and it is. But perhaps even more important is that the President Pro Tempore "shall serve as vice chair of the Rules Committee, and as Chair of the Rules committee during the Lieutenant Governor's absence." The Rules Committee is the final gatekeeper for all other committees, and a vote on Rules is no small vote—because no bill will get to the floor unless it is voted out of Rules.

Every chamber in every state has its own rules and procedures and processes. It's a wise lawmaker who takes the time to learn them and use them to reach her goals.

SENATOR KAREN KEISER
PRESIDENT PRO TEMPORE

Here I am sharing the gavel with Senator Rose Franklin, who had previously served as President Pro Tempore, 2018.

KEY TAKEAWAYS

- The rule book used by your chamber is your procedural bible; read it and use it.
- Formal institutional norms and decorum are devices for keeping tempers and arguments under control.
- Killing bills by filing dozens of amendments is a common minority caucus strategy to eat up hours available for bill action with endless debate. Patience is required if you are in the majority.
- Keep an eye on the people in the gallery watching floor action; a surge in attendance is an early warning of what's likely coming up in the next few minutes.

NOTES

1. Washington State Constitution, Article II, Section 10.

2. Washington Legislative Manual, Permanent Rules of the Senate, Rule 2.

CHAPTER 20

You Really Can Change the World

"Be the change you wish to see in the world."
—Mahatma Gandhi

State legislatures have had a reputation for being bulwarks of the status quo, but they are also often called "the laboratories of democracy." Might they be both?

Efforts to achieve significant change had mainly focused at the federal level for decades, whether through the Oval Office, the Supreme Court, or Congress. But a paradigm shift took shape in the George W. Bush administration when several progressive groups began to develop a focus on training and connecting with state legislators. During the Obama years, progressive state legislators were officially invited to support the president's agenda, from passage of the Affordable Care Act to the Paris Climate Accord.

President Obama had begun his career in the Illinois State Legislature, and he installed an outreach program to link his White House to progressive legislators in the states. I was honored to serve as a cochair of the Working Group of State Legislators that worked with White House liaison Nick Rathod while health reform was being formulated and debated in Congress. In 2009, in fact, we were able to win a vote of support for a Public Option in the Affordable Care Act at the NCSL Convention in Pennsylvania.

But that was then. Since the onset of the Trump administration, the vital necessity of progressive state legislative action has never been clearer. From the promise to "Repeal and Replace" Obamacare, to climate denial and pulling out of the Paris Climate Accord, to the destruction of a fair process for amnesty and immigration—not to mention the rollback of rules to protect consumers and workers at every federal agency—the deconstruction of all things Obama has been an overriding agenda of the Trump administration. The pendulum didn't simply swing, it was sent into a tailspin.

Since the beginning of the battles to restrict the civil rights of African Americans, the banner of state's rights had been raised as a battle cry and a way to deny Black Americans the right to vote, to attend integrated schools, and to ride in the front of the bus. For years, any assertion of state's rights was scorned by good liberals as a back-door path to the horrific era of segregation and lynchings in the Deep South, and many federal laws were passed with preemption clauses to deny states the ability to pass legislation that could exempt them from the federal imperatives.

In addition, businesses lobbied successfully for a uniform code across all states. For example, the federal Employee Retirement Income Security Act includes a broad preemption to limit state laws pertaining to private employer-provided health care benefits or retirement plans. That law limits states from enacting a universal health care system because such a large part of our health care is provided through employer-provided health insurance. Similarly, the federal Arbitration Act preempts state limits on nondisclosure agreements or any contract requiring mandatory arbitration—and that's a lot of contracts, including nondisclosure agreements on sexual harassment and assault. For years the federal government was relied upon to uphold standards of fairness and decency. But that safeguard has been turned upside down, creating a ceiling rather than a floor.

Our federal government, including our federal courts, became captive to conservative ideologues and deep-pocketed billionaires who have remade the federal agenda to serve their far-right goals. From abortion rights to enforcement of the Clean Water Act to the oversight of the National Labor Relations Board, our federal government and court system can no longer be relied on either to enact programs to help working families or to protect those households from the dismantling of existing protections. New federal leadership may be able to restore some of these losses but, in my view, we can't just wait and hope. We can act. Once the federal leadership changes, we can coordinate our efforts.

So what's a progressive to do? Run for the state legislature!

In the past twenty years, I have witnessed a blossoming of innovative and landmark legislation that has improved the lives of residents in many states, especially in blue states but also in some purple states.

In the West, the states of California, Oregon, Washington, Colorado, Hawaii, Nevada, and New Mexico have learned from each other's efforts and successes in passing new progressive programs and laws. A few organizations, such as the State Innovation Exchange (SiX)[1] and the Public Leadership Institute, actively focus on strategizing with state legislators and sharing progressive state legislation.

It is difficult work, under-resourced and under-appreciated, but the successes are substantive. At the same time, the gains are little heralded or celebrated, as the media prefer to focus on federal dysfunction and conflict rather than the steady progress achieved at the state level. The evidence is clear if you look at any national rankings of the states, whether the measure is health status, environmental standards, education rankings, or union density and incomes. Those states that enact progressive state laws score higher on nearly every measure. That means tens of millions of Americans have healthier lives and better futures in those states.

Progressives have a lot to show for our efforts. Consider this "baker's dozen" list of state initiated and enacted laws that further social justice, health care, environmental progress, and workers' rights:

1 **Abortion Rights.** State-guaranteed reproductive rights have been enacted in many progressive states by law or by initiative. The U.S. Supreme Court's Dobbs ruling makes these state actions protecting reproductive rights especially important. Oregon became the first state to mandate that all private insurance plans cover abortion services in 2017. Within three years, six more states had followed suit, establishing protections for 25 percent of the reproductive age women in our country. Since the Dobbs decision, many states have become even more active on abortion rights and funding.

2 **Clean Energy.** Goals to reach ambitious clean energy standards have been adopted in nine states, beginning with Hawaii in 2015. Passing a 100 percent renewable portfolio standard requires all utilities within a state to derive 100 percent of their electricity from renewable resources. Since 2017, some thirty states have passed some variation of the 100 percent renewable standard with varying implementation timelines.

3 **Conversion Therapy Ban.** The harmful practice of subjecting minors to so-called conversion therapy to try and alter their sexual orientation or gender identity has been banned by twenty-one states, with California first in 2012. Other states include Colorado, Connecticut, Delaware, Hawaii, Illinois, Maine, Maryland, Massachusetts, Minnesota, Nevada, New Hampshire, New Jersey, New Mexico, New York, Oregon, Rhode Island, Utah, Vermont, Virginia, and Washington. North Carolina has enacted a partial ban.

4 **Immigration.** The harsh and hateful treatment of undocumented workers has incited fear among many communities of color. One way to address

this fear is to pass city ordinances and state laws to prohibit state and local law enforcement from using funds or resources to "investigate, interrogate, detain, detect or arrest persons for immigration enforcement purposes." Oregon was the first state to pass this sanctuary law, back in 1987. States that have followed suit include Connecticut, Vermont, California, Illinois, and Washington.

5 Minimum Wage Increase. A few years ago, the idea of a fifteen-dollar minimum wage seemed like pie in the sky. But after a local initiative for airport workers passed in 2013 for the city of SeaTac, Washington, the movement has taken off, and many more cities and states have taken action to establish a fifteen-dollar minimum wage. By 2020, seven states and the District of Columbia had passed a fifteen-dollar-an-hour minimum wage standard with various implementation timelines.

6 Paid Sick Leave. Connecticut became the first state to pass a law requiring paid sick days for private-sector employees in 2011. In 2014, California and Massachusetts adopted paid sick day policies. By 2020, fourteen states had adopted paid sick day laws, three of them in response to the coronavirus pandemic.

7 Vote by Mail and Automatic Voter Registration. Rightwing lawmakers and groups have levied unsubstantiated allegations of voter fraud for years in order to impose racist, discriminatory voter ID restrictions on citizens in many red states. Now blue states are pushing back. In 2015, Oregon passed the first automatic voter registration (AVR) statute, automatically registering eligible voters when they receive their driver's licenses. By 2020, sixteen states had some form of AVR. With the coronavirus pandemic, in-person voting can be downright dangerous; vote-by-mail offers an efficient, fair alternative. Washington was the first state to implement universal vote-by-mail in 2012. Colorado, Oregon, Utah, California, and Hawaii have also adopted universal vote-by-mail, and several more states have passed laws to make absentee voting more available.

8 Pregnancy Accommodations. Laws requiring employers to accommodate pregnant employees' health needs have been passed in several states, and could provide a bridge for more conservative states to enact some form of worker's rights. These needs range from seating, restroom breaks, and access to drinking water, and may include a temporary, common-sense shift from heavy- to light-duty work during the later stages of a pregnancy. Tennessee passed a pregnancy accommodation law for state employees in 2018. New York, New Jersey, and Washington have passed broader statutes applying to private sector employers.

9 Prison Gerrymandering. The unfair, longstanding practice of listing an inmate's residence as a prison site rather than a hometown or city has given communities with prisons extra and unjustified representation in census counts. Six states have passed laws eliminating this practice, and more bills have made progress in the state legislatures of Illinois, Pennsylvania, Rhode Island, Texas, Oregon, Louisiana, and New Jersey.

10 Undocumented Driver's License. Denying undocumented immigrants the ability to acquire a driver's license is a punitive policy that undercuts migrant workers and their employers and renders immigrants fearful of reporting traffic accidents and crimes such as thefts and assaults. Twelve states now allow undocumented immigrants to get a driver's license or a state ID card, including Colorado, Connecticut, Delaware, Hawaii, Illinois, Maryland, Nevada, New Mexico, Utah, Vermont, and Washington.

11 Health Care. Once the Supreme Court made the Medicaid expansion in Obamacare optional, only thirty-two states opted to expand the health coverage to citizens with an income of up to 138 percent of poverty. This enabled eighteen states to refuse to extend health care under Medicaid, which is federally subsidized, to millions of low-wage workers in their states.

12 Expanded EITC. Three states enacted a state Earned Income Tax Credit in 2017, for a total of twenty-nine state EITC programs. Twenty-three of those states made the EITC refundable, meaning a poor family may receive a check if their credit exceeds their state income tax liability.

13 Marijuana Decriminalization. Arrests for marijuana possession in states that have legalized marijuana have dropped to near zero, and thousands of people convicted of marijuana possession have been released from prison. Eleven states have legalized recreational cannabis, including Alaska, Colorado, Illinois, Vermont, Oregon, Michigan, Maine, Maryland, Nevada, California, and Washington. In addition, medical marijuana is legal in Arizona, New Mexico, Utah, Montana, North Dakota, Minnesota, Oklahoma, Missouri, Arkansas, Louisiana, Florida, Ohio, West Virginia, Pennsylvania, New York, Delaware, Rhode Island, Connecticut, New Hampshire, and New Jersey.

States have led on progressive issues for so many other fronts as well, from paid family and medical leave to hate crimes and sexual harassment. While a state-by-state approach isn't ideal or as sweeping as federal action, it nevertheless has provided rights and benefits to tens of millions of Americans. Still, a patchwork system of state standards and laws make for a bumpy road in our nation's progress.

One might hope the passage of progressive, similar laws by half a dozen or more states would provide the inspiration to redirect political resources and pass comparable legislation at the federal level. But with our divided federal government at an impasse for several years now, it seems extraordinarily optimistic to put much faith into congressional action on behalf of working families. We can hope that when the federal government, the White House, Congress, and the Courts are restored to some level of functionality, the experiences in our progressive states can serve as examples for federal efforts to provide comparable rights and benefits to all Americans.

In the meantime, the progress in blue and purple states is creating a bifurcation in the living standards across our country. Progressive states that increase minimum wages, health care benefits, environmental standards, civil rights (and more) are creating a healthier, more equal and prosperous society, in sharp contrast to states that decline to act. The impact on people's lives is significant because many progressive states have growing populations and many more people are therefore able to benefit from policies that support their health, education, working conditions, environment, and general welfare. With our nation already suffering from broad wage inequality and differing levels of benefits, any new disparities will only add salt to worsening wounds.

Perhaps the stronger economies and healthier societies of states like Massachusetts, Maryland, Connecticut, California, Colorado, Hawaii, Minnesota, Oregon, Washington, and Nevada will spur envy or resentment. But it would be more productive to spread hope and aspiration for a better future to all the states. Whatever it takes, I am hopeful the examples of progressive state legislation will inspire a level of awareness and action in all states to achieve real change that results in a healthier, wealthier, and less divisive population for us all.

You see, you actually can change the world—even if it happens one state at a time.

KEY TAKEAWAYS

- Never underestimate the honor of being elected to represent your constituents. As their representative, you are dutybound to do your best to improve their lives in any way you can.
- Don't play small ball. Aim your power, influence, and abilities to achieve real, lasting change.
- Build your alliances. Look to other states, state lawmakers, and national and local advocates, and incorporate everything you can into your cause. If you fall short, adapt and repeat.
- Push for federal standards to allow states to do even more on climate, environment, health care, labor, voting rights, discrimination, harassment, and affirmative action.

NOTES

1. Director Anthony Glad and SiX Research Team, State Innovation Exchange, SiX Research Memorandum, May 6, 2020.

CHAPTER 21

A Case In Point

"This is a big fucking deal."
—Vice President Joe Biden on the day the ACA was signed into law in 2010

The Affordable Care Act (ACA) offers probably the most dramatic example of how (though today's Congress may be gridlocked) state legislatures are not gridlocked.

More than a century ago, communities relied predominantly upon local and state officials for solutions to their problems. That all changed when the Great Depression starved communities and states of the resources to do much of anything and, under Franklin Delano Roosevelt, the federal government took the lead in providing the services and assistance to get the country back on its feet.

Politics is often described as a pendulum, although since the Reagan revolution it has mostly swung to the right. In recent years, as the polarization of the electorate has paralyzed Congress, progressives in many states have sought to take the initiative. And nowhere has this been more evident than in the efforts to reform the nation's health care system.

As chair of the Senate Health Care Committee when President Obama was elected in 2008, I was thrilled to be in the right place at the right time to work on progressives' long-sought goal of health reform. Six months into Obama's first term, his White House Office of Intergovernmental Affairs led by Nick Rathod reached out to some thirty state legislators. Through the help of the Progressive States Network—a precursor organization to the State Innovation Network—we organized to recruit other state lawmakers to sign on to a letter to Congress endorsing a robust public option. Some 1,056 state lawmakers from all fifty states signed that letter.

Our core *Working Group of State Legislators for Health Reform*[1] organized at the NCSL Convention in Philadelphia that year to lobby for and win passage of a formal NCSL policy of support. It stated: "We support a program with the following characteristics: It should include a public insurance option side-by-side with commercial insurance for those for whom private insurance is not the best option."

By November of 2009, we were communicating directly through personal visits and letters to members of Congress, urging support of a public option and opposition to the so-called "choice compact" in the Senate. I personally traveled at my own expense to Washington, DC, that year for several meetings at the White House and with members of Congress. Health care reform was being written, and we wanted to influence the outcome because the states would be charged with implementing the law. It was an exhilarating time to participate in the creation of such a huge legislative milestone. I felt it was equivalent to being a part of—and witness to—the 1960s' creation of Medicare and Medicaid. We organized a core group of tough, experienced legislators who kept working until the Affordable Care Act passed Congress on March 21, 2010. Then, for the next four years, the Working Group continued to collaborate on implementation of the law in our respective states.

Here I am greeting President Barack Obama at Boeing Field in Seattle, 2010. I worked with his administration to pass the Affordable Care Act.

Since that victory, we've had a decade-long struggle to defend and expand the Affordable Care Act (ACA), nicknamed Obamacare after the president who signed it into law. Given relentless Republican efforts to shrink, restrict, and reverse the law's reforms through court challenges and legislative actions, the surest protections and advances in health care coverage have taken place—especially in Washington state—in the state legislatures.

Once Congress passed the ACA, it was up to the states to implement it. And while some states struggled, Washington state quickly became recognized as the national leader in implementation.

Our success was no accident.

In 2011, our legislature passed three key bills I'd sponsored to ensure smooth implementation of the ACA. The first, SB 5445, created the state Health Benefit Exchange and set up its partnership structure. The second, SB 5371, required insurance be available to anyone under age nineteen without application of preexisting conditions, reflecting new ACA requirements. The third, SB 5122, modified health care regulation statutes, reflecting new ACA health insurance regulations. This included raising the age of dependents to twenty-six, removing lifetime caps, and expanding independent reviews of appeals.

In 2012, a major bill sponsored by Representative Eileen Cody, HB 2319 lifted restrictions on the state's Health Benefit Exchange, required the Health Benefit Exchange to be self-sustaining, established market rules, codified essential health benefits, and set ACA-compliant rules for catastrophic plans.

In 2013, our legislature followed up with another bill by Cody (HB 1947) that created the funding mechanism for the state's Health Benefit Exchange (HBE) by creating a 2 percent premium tax on HBE plans. And our 2013–2015 biennial budget provided $1.1 billion in federal funding and $312 million in savings towards ACA implementation. It also provided funds to hire staff at the state Health Care Authority.

Republican Senator Curtis King and I in discussion on the floor, 2013.

Then, in 2014, our legislature passed HB 1870 to ensure that key consumer protections would remain in effect for Washingtonians, even if the ACA were to be repealed by the courts or at the federal level. These protections include: prohibiting annual and lifetime caps; removing excessive waiting periods; prohibiting the ability of an insurer to rescind coverage once someone is enrolled; prohibiting preexisting condition exclusions; prohibiting discrimination based on gender, race, national origin, or disability; and mandating coverage of ten essential health benefits, including reproductive care.

The results were dramatic:

- 800,000 state residents gained health care coverage through the state's Health Benefit Exchange and Medicaid expansion.
- The uninsured rate decreased from 14 percent to 5.5 percent (as of 2019).
- 140,000 state residents received subsidized health coverage through the state's Health Benefit Exchange.

Had the Trump administration and congressional Republicans succeeded in their attempts to repeal the ACA, our state would have suffered a huge financial hit. Repeal of the ACA would mean:

- 625,000 state residents would lose Medicaid coverage (based on the loss of $3.6 billion in federal funding).
- 140,000 state residents would lose federal subsidies to purchase health coverage on the Exchange, which would likely mean a loss in coverage because they could no longer afford it.
- The state would lose $620 million in federal subsidies.
- Combined losses to the state would total $4.2 billion in federal funds annually.

Our state passed legislation to ensure that the structure and responsibilities of the Health Benefit Exchange, created by the ACA, are codified in state law. What all this means is that, regardless of anything Republicans may do at the federal level to reduce access to health care coverage, people in Washington state will continue to receive key protections and benefits.

Given the unpredictable pendulum of politics, I'd advise that any progressive victories won in Congress be codified in state statute to ensure that victories don't one day turn into dust.

KEY TAKEAWAYS

- Our state implemented the ACA more smoothly than other states because we laid the groundwork ahead of time, working with the Obama administration and health reform advocates.

- Once the ACA passed and extended a historic level of health care coverage and access to Americans, our state legislature codified the most important of those benefits into state law so that the people of our state will continue to receive those benefits even if they are rolled back at the federal level. Codifying into state statute creates a backstop of protection for states when the political spectrum swings backwards.

- Probably the biggest lesson of all: in today's political environment, states should not (and cannot afford to) wait for Congress to pass laws on behalf of their citizens.

- States can, and should, energetically identify and pass laws that will benefit their citizens regardless of what Congress does.

NOTES

1. Core Working Group members included then-U.S. Representative Kyrsten Sinema, now an Arizona U.S. senator; then-state Senators Jack Hatch (IA) and Dede Feldman (NM); then-state Representative Sharon Treat (ME); state Representatives Garnet Coleman (TX), Verla Insko (NC), and now-state Senator Cindy Rosenwald (NH); then-state Representative and now state Senator Mimi Stewart (NM); former delegates Don Perdue (WV) and Tom Hucker (MD); state Senators. Maggie Carlton (NV), Jon Erpenbach (WI), Nan Orrock (GA), and me. It was my responsibility and privilege to serve as cochair and chair of the Working Group until 2014.

CHAPTER 22

Blue Skies, Dark Clouds

"Pray for the dead and fight like hell for the living."
—Mother Jones

In 2020, Never Trumpers, moderates, liberals, and progressives voted to elect Joe Biden president. But these voters who were so focused on the presidency failed to carry forward their concerns to other branches of government—both the Congressional and the state legislative bodies. The disappointing results paint a contrasting picture of blue skies over the White House and dark clouds over Congress and state capitols.

The election results in 2020 also offer a cautionary tale. The Biden administration got right to work addressing the COVID-19 crisis, and it moved quickly forward on economic stimulus and executive orders reversing scores of policies that had been created by Trump executive orders.

But realists have to face some foreboding facts. In 2022, prognosticators predicted that Republicans would retake the majority in the House, and the Senate majority is so thin it already squeaks. The Senate owes its majority to the remarkable Georgia special election voter turnout. Narrow victories may well be short-lived.[1]

At the state legislative level, eighty-six of the ninety-nine legislative chambers in forty-four states held elections, and Republicans gained majorities in two more chambers. It was the smallest change in partisan legislative control since 1944, when just four chambers changed hands. (Nebraska, as always, is unicameral, controlled by Republican majorities.)[2]

The result is that, in 2021, Republicans controlled thirty legislative assemblies while Democrats held majorities in only eighteen states, with two states splitting control. Twenty-three states now have Republican trifectas, meaning one-party control of both legislative chambers and the governorship; only fifteen states have Democratic trifectas. This freefall for Democratic-held state legislative majorities began in 2010. Before the elections that year, Democrats controlled twenty-seven state legislatures and Republicans just fourteen.

Of course, the 2020 election set the stage for redistricting that shapes the electoral map for the next decade. In state after state, we've seen the fine art of political gerrymandering imposed on distracted voters over the last decade. We've witnessed the results of the 2010 gerrymanders in states such as Wisconsin, where popular votes seem to count for little anymore. In Wisconsin's November 2020 election, Democratic candidates won about 47 percent of total votes in state Senate races but just 38 percent of the seats and hold only twelve of thirty-three seats in the chamber.[3]

What's a democracy to do?

Often we've turned to the courts for recourse. But just imagine what the Supreme Court might do over the next few years! With the court's staunchly conservative six to three majority, the Arizona voting rights case ruling reinforced fears that new limitations on voting will be upheld, and political gerrymandering has already been okayed, abortion rights were overturned federally and will devolve to the states—where all those Republican majorities wait with bated breath.

Indeed, dark clouds lie ahead. But there is a path forward. State legislators can act to protect and improve the lives of tens of millions of Americans, one state at a time. It will take concerted strategy, coordination, and a good deal of money. But we can do this.

KEY TAKEAWAYS

- Long-term strategies to win majorities in state legislatures need to be developed and implemented.
- Work with what you have and build out from one chamber or one state at a time on well-developed, popular issues with voters.
- Develop alliances across state lines with other state legislators working on similar issues, working with advocates to compare initiatives and coordinate approaches.
- Think regionally, with clusters of states in the West, Northern Midwest, and Northeastern states to coordinate and share victories.

NOTES

1. Joan Walsh, "The 7,383 Seat Strategy," *The Nation*, September 7, 2014. https://www.thenation.com/article/archive/the-7383-seat-strategy/.

2. Ballotpedia.org, May 15, 2021, Election Results 2020, State Legislatures that Changed Party Control.

3. Sally Reed, "Gerrymandered districts helped GOP stay in power in state legislature, new analysis shows." *TheBadgerHerald.com*, November 9, 2020.

EPILOGUE

"This time it feels different" is a refrain from the 2020 Black Lives Matter movement. The cumulative wounds of the death upon death of mostly Black men, some young, some not, has been hammered into our national consciousness. So many names, so many marches—and so many of us are just waking up to the untaught history of racism, exclusion, sexism, and homophobia.

Many white folks are labeled "fragile" for their state of denial or uninformed resistance to Black Lives Matter when they react with slogans such as "All Lives Matter" or argue that discussion of racial factors injects race into an issue where it isn't relevant. White privilege is so prevalent that it is usually unseen by whites but duly noted by people of color. Obvious examples include the privilege of walking into a room and not being the only person there of your race—indeed, feeling that the presence of white people in a room is natural and the presence of someone of color is distinct from our societal norm. Or shopping without being tailed by a suspicious salesclerk. Or not fearing for your physical safety, or even your life, when a police officer pulls you over.

Cell phone videos are changing the way we see things, forcing us to become aware of things that we never realized had been happening all too often. This is a profound shift in our collective comprehension—but consciousness raising isn't good enough. Awareness is only the first step. As Bill Fletcher Jr. advises, "Let us not move to easy answers that dodge the more difficult questions." As a people, we must have a reckoning with racism.

Southern states may have created the state's rights paradigm as a racist construct to maintain white dominance. But progressive activists and policy makers can destroy that paradigm with a state-by-state movement that turns that construct on its head.

Marches for racial justice all over the country seem to draw as many white folks as Black folks. Conversations about reconciliation and reparations are happening. And, for once, it appears white folks are listening. But listening and understanding aren't enough. Endless conversations and demonstrations, marches for justice, and internet memes may feel like change, but feelings don't last.

As Ibram X. Kendi concludes in *How to be an Antiracist*, "Success. The dark road we fear. Where antiracist power and policy predominate. Where equal opportunities and thus outcomes exist between equal groups. Where people blame policy, not people, for societal problems."[1]

Getting the 1965 Voting Rights Act enacted was an achieved aim of the civil rights movement activism led by Dr. Martin Luther King Jr. But as King set forth in his book, *Where Do We Go from Here: Chaos or Community?*, we must continually work for policy change. In 1967, King concluded: "I am now convinced that the simplest approach will prove to be the most effective—the solution to poverty is to abolish it directly by: the guaranteed income." In 2020, this idea was resurrected when presidential candidate Andrew Yang made the guaranteed income a centerpiece of his campaign.

"This time it feels different" may be true. I hope it is. But for me, the 2020 Black Lives Matter movement imparts a haunting feeling of déjà vu.

I was a student at University of California, Berkeley when free speech protests, the women's movement, the antiwar movement, and the civil rights movement of the 1960s all converged and shifted the paradigm for the rest of the century. That was when I transformed myself into an activist and feminist. At the time, we thought we had changed the world, but looking back, we failed to build on the gains we made or even maintain them.

Indeed we have been pushed backward on many issues, such as reproductive rights, voting rights, and affirmative action. The growing cancer of income inequality is eating away at our social contract. The election of President Obama allowed us a few minutes to congratulate ourselves on a high-profile moment of racial progress, but Obama's sharing a beer with Henry Gates on the White House lawn after the Black professor had been arrested on his own porch did nothing to end police harassment or address the horrific realities of racism.

So this time it must be different. We must keep pushing on and persisting and insisting. A backlash is probable, along with predictable setbacks. But I have faith and hope that collective effort, practical strategies, and our shared progressive vision will move key states and, hopefully, our county toward that fabled "Promised Land." As Martin Luther King Jr. advised, "The arc of the moral universe is long, but it bends towards justice."

NOTES

1. Ibram Kendi, *How to be an Antiracist*. New York: One World, 2019, p. 218.

BIBLIOGRAPHY

Baily, Kevin, Bob Locander, and Richard Shaw. *How Texas Politics Really Works.* Dallas: Lone Star Productions, 2017.

Carville, James. *We're Right, They're Wrong: A Handbook for Spirited Progressives.* New York: Random House, 1996.

Feldman, Dede. *Inside the New Mexico Senate: Boots, Suits, and Citizens.* Albuquerque: University of New Mexico Press, 2014.

Gerzon, Mark. *The Reunited States of America: How We Can Bridge the Partisan Divide.* Oakland: Koehler Publishers, Inc., 2016.

Heifetz, Ronald A., and Marty Linsky. *Leadership on the Line: Staying Alive through the Dangers of Leading.* Brighton: Harvard Business School Press, 2002.

Horn, Bernie, and Gloria Totten. *Voicing Our Values: A Message Guide for Policymakers and Advocates.* Washington, DC: Public Leadership Institute, 2019.

Hughes, John C., and Bob Young. *Ahead of The Curve: Washington Women Lead the Way, 1910–2020.* Olympia: Washington Office of the Secretary of State, Legacy Washington, 2019.

Jayapal, Pramila. *Use the Power You Have: A Brown Woman's Guide to Politics and Political Change.* New York: The New Press, 2020.

Kantor, Jodi, and Megan Twohey. *She Said: Breaking the Sexual Harassment Story That Helped Ignite a Movement.* London: Penguin Press, 2019.

Kendi, Ibram X. *How to be an Antiracist.* New York: One World, 2019.

King, Martin Luther, Jr. *Where Do We Go From Here: Chaos or Community?* Boston: Beacon Press, 1968.

Meacham, Jon. *The Soul of America: The Battle for Our Better Angels.* New York: Random House, 2019.

Monahan, Dan, ed. *Helen Sommers: An Oral History, 1973–2009.* Olympia: Washington State Legislature Oral History Program, 2010.

Moncrief, Gary F., and Peverill Squire. *Why States Matter: An Introduction to State Politics.* 2nd Edition. Lanham, MD: Rowman & Littlefield, 2017.

Nimura, Tamiko. *Rosa Franklin: A Life in Heath Care, Public Service, and Social Justice.* Olympia: Washington State Oral History Program, 2019.

Oluo, Ijeoma. *So You Want To Talk About Race.* New York: Hachette Book Group, 2018.

Reich, Robert B. *The Common Good.* New York: Alfred A. Knopf, 2018.

Scott, George William. *A Majority of One: Legislative Life.* Seattle: Civitas Press, 2002.

Steinhauer, Jennifer. *The Firsts: The Inside Story of the Women Reshaping Congress*. Chapel Hill: Algonquin Books, 2020.

Vikingstad Valle, Georgette. *Always a Rebel and Never Without a Cause*. Oak Harbor, WA: Blue Sea Publishing, 2007.

GLOSSARY OF COMMON LEGISLATIVE TERMS

Adjourn Sine Die: To conclude a regular or special legislative session without setting a day to reconvene. Sine Die: Latin for "without another day."

Amendment: Any proposed change in a bill, resolution, or memorial. A committee amendment is an amendment proposed in a committee meeting. A floor amendment is an amendment proposed on the floor of a legislative chamber. A striking amendment removes everything after the title and inserts a whole new bill. Amendments can be amended.

Approach the Bar: A legislator's physical movement from any place on the floor of either chamber to the rostrum. Not permitted while a vote is underway.

Appropriation: A legislative allocation of money for a specific purpose.

Appropriations Committee: The chief fiscal committee in the House. The committee is responsible for recommending how state monies will be spent.

Bar of the House or Senate: The rostrum at the front of each chamber—behind which sit or stand the President of the Senate, the Speaker of the House, and others as designated—for presiding over the body, recording, and processing legislation being considered by the chamber.

Bill: A proposed law presented to the legislature for consideration. During a legislative session, many proposed bills are neither heard nor moved.

Boost: A rare legislative procedure on the floor to move a bill directly from its introduction without going through the normal committee hearing process, usually during an extraordinary circumstance.

Bump: Slang term for suspending the rules to allow a bill to be advanced from Second to Third Reading without having the bill revert to the Rules Committee. Generally, to bump a bill is a move that needs bipartisan support.

Calendar: A list or schedule of pending business. Each chamber has many types of calendars: Regular, Consent, Suspension, Concurring, Dispute, Conference, Gubernatorial Appointments, etc.

Call of the House or Senate: A procedure used to compel attendance of all members; if members refuse to attend, they may be arrested.

Call to Order: Notice given indicating the legislature is officially in session. Also used to restore order during floor action.

Capital Budget: Appropriations made to state and local agencies for building and construction projects (infrastructure). Some bodies have separate Capital Budget

Committees; others address capital expenditures within the Appropriations or Ways and Means Committees.

Caucus: The respective groups of Democrats or Republicans in an elective body. The term may be used to refer to the elected officials only or, more broadly, to include staff. Also: the meeting of members of a legislative body who belong to the same political party. Sometimes independents will meet with a specific caucus to learn about bills and issues of concern to the caucus. The Majority caucus and the Minority Caucus each meet behind closed doors and their discussions are considered confidential. The term may be used as both noun and verb, as in "they're in caucus" or "they plan to caucus."

Colloquy: A formal, scripted exchange of questions and answers between members on the floor of the chamber to clarify legislative intent for a bill being considered on the floor.

Committee on Committees: Committees appointed by Leadership in each chamber that meets after elections to select the chairs and members of all the standing committees in the House and Senate.

Companion Bill: A bill introduced in the same form in both the House and the Senate. Often used as a process to show wide support for the proposed legislation.

Confirmation: Approval by the Senate of gubernatorial appointments.

Conflict of Interest: Any interest (financial or otherwise), business or professional activity, or obligation which is incompatible with the proper discharge of duties. Ethics committees or commissions may rule on conflict of interest charges brought against a member.

Cosponsor: A member, or members, who sign onto a bill indicating support for the bill. (New members need to be cautious about cosponsoring bills they don't fully understand, or simply trust the prime sponsor.)

Division: A method of voting on a motion by standing on the floor of the chamber to determine majority without a roll-call vote. Some members sometimes "take a walk" to avoid being counted on some issues.

Division of the Question: Consideration of each item in a bill or motion separately.

Emergency Clause: A provision in a bill that allows a measure to become effective immediately upon the signature of the governor.

Engrossed Amendment: When an amendment has been amended, the changes are worked into the text to create the engrossed amendment.

Engrossed Bill: A bill which reflects all amendments made in the house of its origin.

Ethics: Standard of moral conduct. Legislative ethics standards are set forth in statutes and in House and Senate rules. Members may receive an ethics manual setting forth rulings of an ethics committee from past years and guidance.

Ex officio: Holding one office by virtue of or because of the holding of another office. Ex officio members of a committee may speak but may not vote.

First Reading: First of three readings required to pass a measure. Bills on first reading are introduced and referred to standing committees.

Fiscal Committees: Committees in each house that create budgets, consider revenues, and other financial issues, such as Appropriations, Finance, Capital, Ways and Means, or Transportation committees. Many state fiscal years run from July 1 through June 30.

Fiscal Note: An estimate of the expected cost of a bill to state and/or local government. Fiscal notes are prepared by the affected agencies or a state fiscal office and are considered by fiscal committees to prepare budgets.

Floor Leader: The member elected by the members of the majority caucus to manage and lead floor actions and calendars. The Floor Leader may also direct bills to standing committees and participate in Leadership decisions.

Gerrymandering: Legislative district boundary lines drawn to assert partisan or factional advantages. District boundaries are drawn by a legislative committee in many states. They are drawn by independent commissions in other states, including Washington. District boundaries are redrawn every decade following the national census of population. District populations should not vary by more than 10 percent between districts.

Grandfather Clause: Inserted in a bill making provisions nonapplicable to activities or personnel involved prior to the enactment of the new legislation. Legislative device often used to reach a compromise with stakeholders that will protect past practice but change future practice.

Hopper: A box or tray located in the bill drafting area in which proposed legislative measures are deposited for introduction as a bill. Current practices also allow the filing of bill proposals electronically.

Interim: The time between formal sessions of the legislature. For most states, part time legislatures meet in formal session annually from three to six months. A few states meet only every two years.

Leadership: The group of legislators elected to lead a caucus, including the Speaker of the House, Speaker Pro Tempore, Majority/Minority Leader of the Senate, Senate President Pro Tempore, Floor Leader, Assistant Floor Leader, Deputy Leader, and Caucus Chair. Additional positions may be created for the Leadership team by the Speaker or Leader.

Majority Leader: The leader of the majority party in the state Senate or, in the House, second in command to the Speaker. Elected by the majority caucus in each chamber.

Majority/Minority Bill Reports: Document with members' signatures of a committee recommending a particular action on a bill—in support, opposed, or without recommendation. It is a public record of the committee vote.

Null and Void Clause: Language specifying that a measure is invalid unless funding is provided in the budget by a specified date. A device sometimes used to protect budgets and to undercut costly policy initiatives.

Per Diem: Payment in lieu of living expenses on a daily basis during session. Most lawmakers must pay rent and other expenses while serving in the Capitol while sometimes traveling back home on weekends.

Point of Order: A demand or request by a member for a legislative body to adhere to its rules of procedure. A parliamentary move sometimes used on the floor to dramatically delay or stop action.

Policy Committee: Standing committees focused on policy areas to consider bills in a policy area, such as agriculture, commerce, education, health care, environment, labor, and others.

President Pro Tempore: A senator elected by the full Senate to discharge the duties of presiding officer in the lieutenant governor's absence.

Prime Sponsor: The originator or first name on a bill or amendment that has been introduced.

Pull: Slang term for moving a bill. For example, Rules Committee members may move (pull) bills from the Green sheet to the floor for action by the full Senate or from the White sheet to the Green sheet, or members may vote to pull a bill from a committee to the floor. (Green and White sheets are listings of the bills before they come out of the Rules Committee to the floor.)

Rules Committee: The committee in each chamber responsible for setting the daily floor calendars of the Senate and House. The President of the Senate and the Speaker of the House, respectively, chair these committees. The Rules Committee is the last gate a bill must pass through to be available for floor action.

Rules of the House or Rules of the Senate: Each house has a set of adopted rules for procedures and behaviors. In Washington, members are given a "little red book," as a manual that includes all the rules. The rules can be amended by the body. Every member is given a copy of the rules for their chamber and should read them and watch how they can be used.

Scope and Object: A parliamentary ruling by the presiding officer as to whether a proposed amendment fits within the subject matter of the bill under consideration. Senate and House rules prohibit amendments which change or expand the scope and object of a bill. Legal counsel advises the presiding officer.

Second Reading: The reading of a bill for the second time, in open floor action, allowing for amendments to be proposed, debated, attached, or defeated in floor debate.

Severability Clause: A section of a bill which instructs the court that if one section of the act is found unconstitutional, the remainder of the act will remain intact.

Speaker: Presiding officer of the House of Representatives.

Striking Amendment: An amendment removing everything after the title and inserting a whole new bill. Strikers can be amended; therefore, you might see a designation for Adopted as Amended. The version of the amendment with the changes worked into the text is labeled Engrossed. A striking amendment offered on the floor can be a hostile amendment meant to kill the bill.

Substitute: A version of a bill offered and adopted in a committee in the originating chamber. If adopted, the substitute replaces the original bill or resolution. Substitutes cannot be offered on the floor or by the non-originating chamber.

Third House: An association of lobbyists whose membership includes most of the professional lobbyists in the state who often consider themselves the so-called "Third House" of the legislature.

Third Reading: The final consideration of a bill on the floor of either house. The bill can be debated, tabled, or referred but not amended. Final passage takes a constitutional majority.

Ulcer Gulch: Slang term for area in the Legislative Building used by lobbyists and the general public for telephone calls and messages.

Ways and Means: The chief revenue and appropriations committee in the Senate. The committee is responsible for recommending how state monies will be spent and the means that will be used to raise tax revenues.

Whip: An assistant to the majority or minority leader. The duties of the whip include counting votes, checking attendance, and maintaining caucus discipline on partisan issues and procedural questions. Accuracy and trust are two essential qualities of a whip.

ACKNOWLEDGMENTS

I have so many people to thank for encouraging me and helping me write this book. First and foremost, my heartfelt gratitude goes to my volunteer editor and wonderful adviser Rick Manugian. I met Rick in the Senate where he has worked as a senior communications specialist for the Democratic Caucus for many years and had worked with me some time ago as my caucus communications staffer. Both of us found the time during the pandemic lockdown to get a big start on the project. In our many intermittent weekend and evening emails and phone conferences, Rick gently corrected my syntax and grammar and smartly sharpened my focus and emphasis. After completing the first draft, he took on the slow slog of a second edit. His help was priceless; his encouragement kept me going. I owe Rick a very large debt of gratitude.

So many colleagues, past and present, generously offered their recollections, opinions, and advice, and I thank them for sharing their knowledge and experiences. Senator Rebecca Saldana's sage advice, Senator Jeff Holy's wise observations, Senator Nguyen's perceptive perspectives, and Senators Wilson's and Lovelett's lived experiences were generously shared and greatly appreciated. Representative Eileen Cody, who has actually served in the Washington legislature longer than I have, was an invaluable resource and shared many of her recollections of some of the escapades and gossip we had heard about over the years. I also received wonderful suggestions from many of my newly elected colleagues who offered their thoughts and suggestions.

Finally, I have to thank my kids, who put up with their mom being a politician while they were young teens. They didn't have their mom around for all their events, and sometimes they were even willing to come to some of my events. They've all grown up to be wonderful, independent adults, yet they still allow me to call them "kiddo." When I shared an early draft that included some revealing family history, they agreed sharing our personal story was an important piece of the project.

INDEX

Page numbers in italic refer to illustrations; an n indicates a note.

ABOUT THE AUTHOR

Washington state Senator Karen Keiser has served as Senate President Pro Tempore, Chair of the Senate Labor, Commerce & Tribal Affairs committee, chair of the Senate Health and Long Term Care Committee, and a member of the powerful budget-writing Senate Ways & Means Committee. Representing the 33rd Legislative District in South King County, she was first elected to the Washington state House of Representatives in 1996 and has served in the Senate since 2001. She was elected to the Senate in 2002 and has been re-elected five times.

Prior to becoming a legislator, Keiser worked as communications director of the Washington State Labor Council, AFL-CIO, Seattle from 1981 to 2002. She wrote speeches, news releases, op-eds, and newsletters, and also produced the television show, *Washington Works*, on KBTC-TV Tacoma for four years. She also worked as reporter, producer, and anchor in three television markets—KGW in Portland, KMGH in Denver, and KSTW in Tacoma, from 1971 to 1981. She earned a bachelor's degree in political science and a master's degree in journalism at the University of California, Berkeley, and she is a member of the Phi Beta Kappa society.

Keiser was born and raised in Iowa, and now lives in Des Moines, WA.